EMILY BRONTË
THE ARTIST AS A FREE WOMAN

Stevie
Davies
EMILY BRONTË
the artist as a free woman

Carcanet
Manchester

Published in 1983 by
CARCANET PRESS LIMITED
210 Corn Exchange Buildings
Manchester M4 3BQ

British Library Cataloguing in Publication Data

Davies, Stevie
    Emily Brontë
    1. Brontë, Emily—Criticism and interpretation
    I. Title
    823′ .8   PR4173

ISBN 0-85365-489-7

The publisher acknowledges the financial assistance of
the Arts Council of Great Britian

Typesetting by Anneset, Weston-super-Mare
Printed in England by SRP Ltd., Exeter

to Rosalie
my dear love

Contents

A NOTE ON NAMES

There is a special difficulty attaching both to the naming of the author and of her heroine in *Wuthering Heights*. To refer to Emily Brontë solely by her Christian name may seem presumptuously familiar; by her surname alone not only patriarchal but also confusing (since at least four Brontës were published authors); by both names as unduly cumbersome. I have decided to compromise by making it a general practice to refer to Emily Brontë as 'Emily' when I speak of her personal life; as 'Emily Brontë' when I am concerned with her writings. The problem of making the two Catherines of *Wuthering Heights* distinct for my reader has been solved for the purposes of this book by alluding to the elder as 'Catherine' and the younger as 'Cathy', though this is by no means the author's invariable practice.

PART ONE:

HER LIFE

1 *The Art of Memory*

The papers were yellow with time, all having been written before I was born. It was strange now to peruse for the first time the records of a mind whence mine own sprang; and most strange and to me sad and sweet, to find that mind of a truly fine, pure and elevated order. They were written for Papa before they were married . . . . I wish she had lived and that I had known her.

NINE letters survived the death, at the age of 38, of Emily Brontë's mother. These were cherished over the years by her father, and shown to her elder sister Charlotte who made her first conscious acquaintance with that mind which was the source of her own, in adult life. The poignant sense of elation at finding out the existence of this little hoard of letters salvaged from the past, combined with that faint shock of an encounter with a crucial event which had occurred in that unimaginable period 'before I was born' are movingly conveyed in Charlotte's account. Emily Brontë never saw these letters nor knew of their existence: they were revealed to Charlotte after her sister's death. But in Emily's life and art there is a comparable searching-back to source, to the faded testimony of the past. The elder Catherine's diaries in *Wuthering Heights* are curiously opened and read after her death by Lockwood, lying on her bed. Emily conveys in her novel the excited nostalgia of lying in someone else's place and leafing through the remnants of the past which carry the echo of a life into the future. Emily Brontë had grown up in a large family of semi-orphaned children, without a mother. It was one of the most salient facts of her existence, a crucial absence which initiated a chain of losses which her art tried to redeem.

There was no lack of a father. The Reverend Patrick Brontë's huge life-span and huger personality—he lived from 1777 to 1861—dwarf the mortal brevity of his wife and six children's existences. Like his surviving daughters, he was a published poet, and like them a person of extraordinary energy, tenacity of purpose and an introspective lover of privacy. Emily's surname is a dignified fiction, for her father was born the son of Hugh

3

Brunty—or Prunty—or O'Pronty—depending on how you liked to spell it (in a semi-literate society there is room for pleasant licence in these matters), an Irish peasant farmer. Patrick was the eldest of ten children, born in a one-windowed, thatched, two-roomed cottage in a parish in County Down called Drumballyroney-cum-Drumgooland, a name rich in comical possibilities which would no doubt have delighted the Brontë children. The adaptation of his original surname to 'Brontë', one of the titles of the heroic Lord Nelson, carrying a suggestion of a vaguely exotic and patrician background very creditable to the wearer, was the product of Patrick Brontë's steady rise in the world. From handloom-weaving and the blacksmith's trade, through school-teaching, and a vigorous course of self-education, he hoisted himself up through the social scale, until he could escape Ireland altogether and enrol as a student at St John's College, Cambridge, in 1802. Emily Brontë was therefore blessed with a father who was in himself a sort of embodied social revolution: refusing to accept the lowly status into which he had been born, he had arduously struggled upwards, to shed his class, his country and his condition. He had learned to love books with a passionate enthusiasm engendered by the difficulty of getting access to them, and passed that hunger on to his children, along with an ample personal library to which they could refer freely: an unusual privilege especially for girls, in an age which found part of Virgil and Shakespeare coarsening to the infant, and especially female, mind. As Patrick Brontë fought his class, so Emily Brontë sloughed the restrictions of her sex.

Patrick Brontë was a person of iron views, fiercely Protestant and inclining to the Wesleyan and Evangelical. The individualism which is so deeply embedded in such Protestantism reappeared, in different forms, in all his daughters, but found its most radical form in Emily's insistence on spiritual freedom from any external creed or dogma. As a Celt, he passed on to his children an intensely imaginative and resourceful temperament, and a potential violence of response, being somewhat fond of things military. Patrick Brontë was under no circumstances afraid to appear peculiar or eccentric, and after the loss of his wife his ways became more evidently odd. Many stories were told of his strange behaviour in Haworth, and he very successfully quelled the riotous elements in a traditionally most barbarous congregation through a combination of violent coerciveness and a very real benevolence. A tendency to cranky despotism is evidenced in his alleged burning of the children's little slippers while they were out on a walk (as being overly luxurious pieces of apparatus), and a refusal to have curtains at the windows of the Parsonage for similar draughty reasons. From his intimate experiences of the Luddite rioting in Dewsbury he retained the habit of sleeping with loaded pistols which he would fire off from the window in a regular early-morning ritual: the thunders of which demonic Jehovah no doubt contributed to the prudent respect of his parishioners. Later he taught Emily to shoot, sensing in her a kindred spirit. Her spartan temperament and her hatred of externals are very like those of her father; so is her extraordinary physical courage, her pride and stoicism and her liking for privacy. But Patrick Brontë could also laugh and be tender; he played with his children and talked to them as equals. They discussed from their earliest days the political news; read *Blackwood's Magazine*; were fierce Tories by conviction and interested themselves from the very cradle in the controversies of world affairs. Emily appears to have taken after her father more obviously than any of the other children, including Branwell: for though he inherited his father's red hair ('carroty', as Charlotte said disparagingly), and was the only boy—the favoured heir—in a family of girls, he was small and insignificant in stature, and surrounded by female precocity subverted by no direct maternal pressure into tame habits of mind. Emily stood out as the darkest member in a fair-haired family; the most attractive in a self-consciously plain family; and as being very tall, as her father was, in a family of diminutive people. She shared her father's classic features, and his unusual pale blue eyes, which in her were said to be extremely beautiful. She could happily look down upon her brother and tolerate his opinion of her as one of 'them things' (girls), whose person is 'lean and scant, with a face about the size of a penny', as Charlotte satirically recorded her brother's view.

Patrick Brontë met the woman who was to be Emily's mother in 1812, and married her that same year. He had graduated and entered the ministry; had published his *Cottage Poems* intended for the edification and comfort of the labouring poor of the class he had left, and was 35 years old. His bride, Maria Branwell, was 29 and Cornish, born in Penzance the fifth daughter of Thomas and

Anne Branwell. She left behind a fairly easy, sedate life in the middle-class south of England for the rigours of the industrial north and the comparative hardship and poverty of a clergyman's wife's existence. She seems to have been a strict and self-disciplined person, firm, loving and humorous. One of her letters implies however rather more than this fairly commonplace bundle of qualities, relevant because it suggests some of the seeds of her daughters' prodigal and corporate brilliance and presents an insight into Patrick Brontë's underlying turbulence and sensitivity:

> I really know not what to make of the beginning of your last; the winds, waves and rocks almost stunned me. I thought you were giving me the account of some terrible dream, or that you had had a presentiment of the fate of my poor box, having no idea that your lively imagination could make so much of the slight reproof conveyed in my last. What will you say when you get a *real, downright scolding*?

In reading this beautifully measured tempering of Patrick's eruption of hurt feeling at some imagined slight, by her own dextrous, loving wit, along with the application of 'real, downright' practical reason, buoyantly conveyed in the cadences of an unusually assured prose style, we get an idea of the measure of the deprivation which Maria's bereaved children were to suffer.

Patrick took his wife north to Thornton in the Bradford diocese of Yorkshire, where all her children were born. They moved to Haworth in 1820, where Patrick became perpetual curate of St Michael's Church, Emily being at that time two years old. Patrick was following in the footsteps of the rampant evangelical William Grimshaw in undertaking the curacy of Haworth, where the latter had put into practice his conception of the ministry as a call to keep up a furious physical and spiritual assault on the working man's recalcitrant soul. His love of the working man led him to move heaven and earth to aid the needy; his duty to the working man required him to whip drinkers out of pubs and into churches; to wrestle sinning mortals whom he happened to meet on the moors in the course of his perambulations down onto their knees for a bout of prayer; to pray himself in a mighty trumpeting voice outside the windows of any dying person who refused to have him in to ease his passage from this world to the next: 'At least he will die with the word of God in his lugs'. The congregation at Haworth was a lively and grim one, better thought of as an incipient mob. Taking against Patrick Brontë's immediate predecessor, Samuel Redhead, it mutinied on three successive Sundays. On the first it marched out; on the second it fell about in the pews laughing as a man sitting back-to-front on a donkey with a pile of hats on his head patrolled the aisle; on the third it completed the ritual by introducing a soot-covered chimney-sweep into the service. This individual stood under the pulpit gesturing in an asinine manner throughout the sermon, in ardent agreement with what was being said; then undertook to scale the pulpit with a view to embracing and kissing the preacher, who finally ran for sanctuary in the Black Bull, and departed Haworth in relief.

On 20th April, 1820, Patrick Brontë came to take his place, bringing Maria and their six children to this demanding parish, with all their worldly goods in a wagon and seven carts. Anne, the youngest, was three months old. Once they arrived, they had less than a year to settle before Maria began to show the symptoms of terminal illness. Their new home, a stone-built rectangular house, was exposed on the one hand to the open moors which were to represent 'home' for Emily just as surely as the scoured and neat interior world, and on the other looked down upon the stone slabs of a well-filled and not at all salubrious graveyard. The dead population, labelled and put to bed, slept next to the diminishing population of the Parsonage, which gave up so many of its members in such a brief time to the vault of the church in which Grimshaw had raved and exhorted, and which now enjoyed the more austere but equally dynamic utterances of Patrick Brontë. His wife died of stomach cancer in September, 1821, when Emily was 3 years and 2 months old.

Emily remembered nothing definite about her mother. But it would not be accurate to say that she retained no impression of her mother and the experience of losing her. It is something that would be thrust very deeply down into the unreachable parts of a child's subconscious mind. Maria spent seven months in protracted dying, bearing (as her husband said) 'more agonising pain than I ever saw anyone endure', that is, a sixth of Emily's entire life to that date. All the children were suffering from scarlet fever during that period. One has only to observe a three-year-

·old's demanding, vulnerable, loquacious and questioning behaviour to realize that this first loss—though not recalled consciously—must have affected Emily powerfully, and have been carried with her until her dying day. At the age of 3, when change of any sort is at best a challenge and at worst a disaster, Emily Brontë woke up on the morning of 16th September, 1821, to find that she had no mother: there was no longer any such person on the face of the earth. She was the fifth of six children at the moment of her mother's death. They had all tumbled out into the world in one another's wake, each more or less within a year of one another. The eldest, Maria, was born in 1814; Elizabeth in 1815; Charlotte in 1816 and Branwell in 1817. Emily's birth in 1818 was followed by a fractional pause, and the birth of Anne—who was to become paired with Emily as a sort of 'twin'—in January, 1820. The jostling for place that must have accompanied the rapid accumulation of infant Brontës would have been momentarily quieted at this first great bereavement (though their father, sealed into the mourning silence of a reserve and detachment which from this time grew upon him, recorded that 'the innocent yet distressing prattle' of his children exacerbated his suffering). The installation of the indispensable and pious but not very consolatory or agreeable Aunt Branwell to take their mother's place in the household, also marked a break with the old, lost world. Miss Elizabeth Branwell was a maiden aunt of forty-five, a gentlewoman very set in her ways—and those ways were strictly Calvinistic, punitive and morally astringent—suddenly called upon to take the onus of a large family of six children all under the age of seven; far from home, in the middle of nowhere. It must have been a nightmare for her, but she fulfilled her responsibilities according to the requirements of her code of conduct, earning from the children much respect and gratitude, little love. As a mother-substitute, Aunt Branwell seems to have been perceived as totally inauthentic. Emily's eldest sister, Maria, moved over from the group of children toward the adult world, to stand in the posture of mother to the younger ones, protecting, cherishing and nurturing them. The children in their bereavement became more closely knit, weaving their lives around one another, absorbing the shock and pain on one another's behalf.

The period of Emily Brontë's early childhood is of the most crucial significance for the study of her later life and art, for childhood is the central theme to which she constantly recurs. In *Wuthering Heights,* writing at the age of nearly 28 within three years of her own death, Emily created an art of memory, in which it is revealed that we always contain, and essentially are, the child we once were. It is like looking down into a well. As you look down, you are met by the face of your supposedly outlived self staring back up at you. Such moments of vision catch the characters unawares: they had not known that they were about to look back in this way. It is as if you can fall deep into a dream, in your waking state: there is a door, or window, through to the past, accessible in the mind. The past has the quality of realizing itself in the present moment, so as to be indistinguishable in texture from what passes for current reality. Catherine tells of waking dreams. Nelly suddenly 'sees' Hindley as a tiny boy and her playfellow. No memory is ever lost; no incident or event shed. Character and relationships, for Emily Brontë, are immutable, stable and eternal. They echo and mirror one another. Emily's characters are like envelopes: if you unfold and open them, you can find a message which was written there long ago and placed inside for the future. Sitting at the kitchen table at the Parsonage, Emily and Anne would write on their birthdays 'Diary Papers' addressed to themselves in the future, to be opened at a stated date:

> A PAPER to be opened
> when Anne is
> 25 years old,
> or my next birthday after
> if
> all be well.
> Emily Jane Brontë. July the 30th, 1841.

In these they would note what was going on in the house and in their imaginations; their hopes and plans; the present state of affairs in the Gondal saga—and then these sealed messages would be put away and never looked at until the anniversary. The circumstances and countenances of the writers changed; the message in its sealed and secret envelope, not at all. Personality for Emily Brontë is like this, sealed, fixed, arrested and immutable. You are bounded where your deepest affinities rest; and those affinities are brought into the world with you when you first enter it. There is often some slight shock when reading these scraps of autobiography with their caricature drawings of herself and Anne, at the realization of how childish Emily Brontë continued to be, in habits of mind and behaviour, into her young adult life. She and Anne played the Gondal fantasy game of 'Let's pretend' well into adulthood. This appearance of regression and 'childishness' may be the essential corollary to the positive charge of Emily's perception that the vital sources of our existence are found in the polarities, intuitions, cast of mind, of the child-in-man. In her novel, with a maturely controlled art, she returned us to our origins. Writing *Wuthering Heights* at the age of 27, she also exposed the infant Emily she continuously contained, the girl of 3 years and 2 months who woke one morning to find that she had, unaccountably, no mother. The infant who had remained for 24 years sealed up in the envelope of self had continued to suffer, mourn and wail—like a waif; or a wraith; or like the ghost of Catherine in Lockwood's dream, calling at the window—in exactly the same way, without any extenuation or modification of her emotion. This is why Emily's earliest days deserve our lingering reflection.

Looking back into this earliest period of Emily's existence, for which we have no more direct evidence than the servants' agreement that she had been 'the prettiest of the children', we can perhaps see another reason why the past, forged and moulded by that first loss and its consequences, set fast and directed itself into the future. It could not be discarded because, in the most bizarre way, it repeated itself. It is the most difficult thing in the world to replace a natural mother artificially, as Patrick Brontë found upon making proposals to two suitable females who he ingenuously thought might care to enter into possession not only of his own person but also of the cramped house, unhealthy situation, small income and six small burdens. Elizabeth Firth and Mary Burder (his former fiancée), being afflicted neither with love nor mental deficiency, recognized that they were being invited into a state of consecrated slavery, and declined. The artificial mother he could provide, Aunt Branwell, approximated to the wire-mother rather than the cloth-mother in the modern experiments with orphaned monkeys. Evidently her judicious, disciplinarian and poker-faced principles of applied rectitude could inspire resentment of unusual longevity, for one of the young servants reminiscing in old age (Nancy Garrs) remembered Aunt Branwell's mathematical administering of the servants' daily beer as being very mean, and called her 'so cross-like an' fault-finding an' so close' by contrast to her deceased sister. In her portrait, Aunt Branwell's upright and unyielding disposition is obvious as she sits straight-faced in her chair, certain cork-screw ringlets regimented on either side of an expressionless face in perpetuation of an old fashion for false curls, beneath a lacy bonnet. Her dress is black; her hands handsome and rather strong. This funereal appearance, and the known rigour of her religious views—so bracing to the holder, so worrying to the vulnerable mind of the hearer, such as Anne, who had to sleep with her—might inspire respect but not tenderness. This wire-mother thus presided over a household of tumultuous infants, rampaging, boisterous, needy, searching, unruly, breaking out on a regular basis into the colds, rashes and nameless viruses that so effectively prevent the Paradisal aspects of childhood from overwhelming us. (*Wuthering Heights* is punctuated with realistic accounts of childhood illness, reinforcing our sense of the validity and unselectiveness of Emily's memory of childhood.) The smaller children in their new condition of emotional nakedness turned to the 'cloth-mother', Maria, for comfort, and she, being to hand, and seeing the problem, lifted them all onto her seven-year-old shoulders, and bore the weight of her Atlas burden with gentleness and composure. Emily could renew her trust here, in the three years between her mother's death and the second wave of loss when she was sent away to school in 1824.

Aunt Branwell made a school-room of her bedroom, and there she had the children sewing samplers with improving texts; and reading religious pamphlets. Emily's probable resistance to having her mind purified in this manner may be imagined from her account of Catherine and Heathcliff's hurling their loathed copies of *The Helmet of Salvation* (which they clearly wished to avoid wearing) and *The Broad Way To Destruction* (on which they had conscientiously embarked) into the dog-kennel, observing that they hated a good book. Though it is highly unlikely that Emily in her childhood engaged in throwing books (there was strict discipline in Aunt's bedroom, and no reputation for active mutiny on Emily's part has reached us), her mind registered a constitutional and violent intolerance of propaganda as well as a strong sense of the ridiculous. The wicked sense of humour she directs against Joseph's sham piety in *Wuthering Heights* as he gloats over the progress of the 'ill childer' down the broad high way that leads to destruction, must have been growing since her earliest days. It is a painless way of aborting any growth of alien ideas preying on her mind, and a way of guarding her originality. Her sense of humour is an aspect of that tenacious reserve with which she defended her integrity from an early age. Emily learned to sew, clean, bake marvellous bread, nurse the ill and manage a house. She was by nature intensely practical, and good at these tasks. She learned to read well (her school register at Cowan Bridge remarked that, on entry, she 'works a little and reads very prettily') and devoured everything legible; but was oddly backward at writing, and never learned to write an elegant hand. She must have been very concerned to form individual judgements in assessing the world around her from an early age, for she was thoroughly impervious to convention all her life. Always, she was terse and pithy in utterance, the soul of brevity. You can feel this ruthless linguistic economy in *Wuthering Heights* where there is hardly a wasted word. She was increasingly quiet or mute in company, except that of her family, so that she must have listened, mused over, inwardly mocked, sorted and savoured the details of everyday life—servants talking, the household, the church and village—in a peculiarly inward way. Her sewing was poor, and the obligatory samplers terminating in the relief of 'Emily Jane Brontë: Finished this Sampler April the 22nd. 1828' give the impression of having been fashioned by a savage process of jabbing with a needle. There is a sense of an unusually stern, rational, ironic and free-thinking child, an impression which is endorsed by a fragment of her talk which Mrs Gaskell preserved as told to her by Patrick Brontë after all his children were dead. Emily was perhaps six when her father, on a characteristically brilliant intuition, assembled his children in his study to elicit their feelings by putting key questions to them which must be answered standing behind a mask. Behind the mask, the child, intact and secure in an assumed anonymity, could afford to tell the truth. A mask would be perfect for Emily, who so deeply held back from personal exposure. Her father wanted to know from her what course of action should be followed when Branwell misbehaved. Emily's prescription for her volatile brother's tantrums was

'Reason with him, and when he won't listen to reason, whip him'. This is clearly the answer of a rationalist who hopes for the best, and a realist acquainted with the intransigence of human nature; also, perhaps, the reply of a little girl who is tired of having her absorbing games spoilt by the antics of a bellowing boy.

One of the last recorded experiences before leaving Haworth for school was the Crow Hill bog burst of 2nd September, 1824. The three eldest girls had already been removed, and Emily (recovering from whooping cough before joining them) was standing on the verge of the next series of losses. Anne, Branwell, Emily and the two servants were out for a walk on the moors when Patrick Brontë standing at his window became aware of an ominous stilling and darkening of the air, followed by the uproar of a huge storm accompanied by earth tremors which shook the whole surrounding countryside. The bog above Ponden burst through its peaty crust and avalanched down the hill, forcing boulders before it. Patrick was terrified on his children's account: it seemed to him standing helplessly at the window that they could not have survived. However, they had taken cover, and Patrick was able to relieve his feelings by putting the incident into a stirring sermon on Divine power and providence. It is likely that Emily, whose reaction to storms and earthquakes was one of excitement untainted by anxiety, put the incident into store in her mind as an emotional and spiritual resource. The souls of Catherine and Heathcliff in *Wuthering Heights* are, they think, 'made of' lightning.

Two months later, at the age of 6 years and 3 months, Emily joined her three elder sisters at the Clergy Daughters' School at Cowan Bridge, which Charlotte Brontë so eloquently described in *Jane Eyre* as a kind of penitentiary to which unsuspecting and impoverished parents might care to yield up their innocent lambs to hunger, suffer and to die. The idea animating the founder of the school, the Reverend Carus Wilson, was that by scourging the bodies it might be possible to save the souls of sinful children. The school was inefficiently run, cold, its régime inhumane, the children more often than not tired, hungry, ill and abused. Maria, the patient eldest Brontë, who was only 10½ when she arrived, seems to have been singled out for especially punitive treatment, owing to the transparently evil constitution of her spirit manifest to those trained to diagnose such things. Charlotte, and later

Emily, had to watch their beloved sister, the deepest source of
solace and security they had, persecuted and tormented by a
grossly ignorant establishment. Charlotte's desperate anger never
died in her; Emily's reaction was mute, but probably very deep.
Though, as the baby of the school, she may have been petted and
therefore defended from the worst excesses of the school régime, at
a mere six years old she was in no fit state to be exiled from her
home. The first unrepeatable catastrophe of the loss of her
mother, scarcely yet covered over by the strata of new experiences,
was exposed and reiterated. On 6th May, 1825, Maria was dead of
tuberculosis; on 15th June, Elizabeth too was dead, Charlotte and
Emily having been fetched home. Emily's total residence of 6
years and 10 months in the world had issued in desertion on an
immeasurable scale, during which the universe might well have
seemed to turn 'to a mighty stranger'. In a place of exile and
deprivation, she had lost her second 'mother', the little girl of
eleven who stood between the smaller children and their losses.
Love had been seen to be powerless; maternity an ineffective
guarantor of shelter, undermined by mortality. The three losses,
seeming to mirror one another, must have seemed to partake of an
eternal condition, with which she must be at war. They
threatened the roots of value and existence. For the rest of Emily's
life, moving away from Haworth was associated with death. The
path to the outside world led directly to a funeral—the treble
funeral in which the elder sisters went down to join their mother.
When she went to Roe Head School in 1835, at the age of 17, she
began palpably to decline and die. Charlotte found friends there,
made some adaptation, and was able to acquire some useful skills,
but Emily had become incapable of transplantation:

> Liberty was the breath of Emily's nostrils; without it, she
> perished. The change from her own home to a school, and
> from her own very noiseless, very secluded, but unrestricted
> and inartificial mode of life, to one of disciplined routine
> (though under the kindliest auspices) was what she failed in
> enduring. Her nature proved here too strong for her
> fortitude. Every morning when she woke, the vision of home
> and the moors rushed on her, and darkened and saddened
> the day that lay before her. Nobody knew what ailed her but
> me—I knew only too well. In this struggle her health was

quickly broken: her white face, attenuated form, and failing strength threatened rapid decline. I felt in my heart she would die if she did not go home, and with this conviction obtained her recall.

Charlotte's description (written with such urgency and immediacy though Emily had been two years dead, and the occasion was now 15 years in the past) tells of Charlotte's own panic that Emily would go, according to a nightmare logic, the way of Maria and Elizabeth. Emily stayed three months, came home, revived. At Brussels in 1842, where she went to school at the Pensionnat Héger with Charlotte at Aunt Branwell's expense, in order to train for teaching and open a school, Emily managed a full nine months away from home in a state of intense stress but determined not to disgrace herself again; after which gestation she returned home thankfully to be reborn in her own image. The description of the terrified, mute young woman in Brussels, clinging on to Charlotte's arm as they walked round the school playground amongst the seething chattering crowds of girls, happily fashionable and light-minded, resembles nothing so much as a young child hanging on to its mother for protection. But Emily by then was 24 years old. The children with whom she studied and whom she taught heartily disliked her. Throughout her life, she never made a single friend of her own outside her family, as though to move past blood-kin might prove lethal. She was, and knew that she was, a misfit. Clinging to Charlotte, in this attitude of helplessness, she is revealed in her weakness. It was as if she feared throughout her life that the crowding human race, shouldering in upon her, was a force for bereavement. As one of its major themes, *Wuthering Heights* has the figure of a lost, exposed and homeless child as a kind of corporate image for the human condition. The author turns a magnificently analytical, ordering mind upon the sources of her own distress. Mother-figures in the novel are absent, briefly present or substituted for, tending to die in labour, or off the map. Catherine dies in childbirth, but her posthumous presence dominates the second half of the book: the ghost of her childhood is reflected in the presence of the daughter who shares her name. Heathcliff has no mother at all, and Catherine fears that without him, the universe would turn to 'a mighty stranger'. 'Stranger' is the most frightening word of all in

Emily Brontë's vocabulary: it represents the meeting, in person, with our primal losses. It is said that she was unable to look a stranger in the eyes, but would be caught constantly in an attitude of turning away from anyone who looked her in the face. Unknown or even slightly known people had for her the character of foreigners, and if anyone came upon her in Haworth or on the moors and spoke to her, she would not meet his eyes. The tendency of her life, from the time of Cowan Bridge on, was to retreat from external confrontation to the 'bright eyes' of her visions, the kind eyes of her family, who fended off strangers for her. Charlotte at nine years old the eldest remaining daughter, stepped into the again vacant position as 'mother' to the others, but that place could never again be filled by one of their own line. Its occupational hazards seemed too demonstrably real.

Wuthering Heights is a novel rich in substitutions, a gift for making which is a great aid to survival, since its precious art enables the loser to transfer value to some existing object which either resembles or derives from what has been lost. We have seen Emily in a posture of weakness; but the truth is that she was, most powerfully, a survivor, who knew where the boundaries of her security might lie, and how to exercise her extraordinary energies, aptitudes and personal bravery within them. In her art, out of the first Catherine who will not survive because she cannot adapt, she draws the second Catherine, who will and can. Her novel is a myth of resurrection, renewal, a fresh start; and her art is therefore essentially recreative and tragi-comic. For an absence, she can supply a presence, evolved out of and germane to a situation of loss. Given motherless children within her novel—and almost all the characters are, including rootless, urban, effete Lockwood— she supplies a universal mother, Ellen, servant and narrator, nurse, guardian, care-taker, know-all, twinned to Hindley (they were born on the same day) and married only to the material of the story. Ellen cared for the first Catherine and the second in their childhoods; she fostered Heathcliff, however reluctantly; nursed Linton on his deathbed and Lockwood in his illness. There is an important precedent for this magic art of recreation and re-rooting, so that human nature can get a local grip on the unyielding substance of the mortal world which must be its home, in Emily's early childhood. It came just before the departure to Cowan Bridge, in the form of Tabitha Aykroyd, to whose care the six-year-old Emily could return in June, 1825.

With Tabby came an expanding sense of being rooted in a locality—the moors and countryside around Haworth, its history, gossip, pagan superstitions, folklore and scandals. Tabby was a widow of 56 when she came as a servant to the Brontës: Emily had left for Cowan Bridge later than her sisters, presumably because of the debilitation caused by whooping cough, so that with Anne, who at the tender age of 4 was too young to be sent out into the cold air of the outside world, and with Branwell, Emily was the first to benefit from Tabby's care. Patrick Brontë took an elderly servant because they came so cheap: thrift was always a guiding motive when any changes had to be considered. Tabby spoke a rich, satiric, harsh and warming Yorkshire dialect. She told stories of the supernatural able to make a person's hair stand on end; and remembered back to the primitive, violent times of the 1780s and '90s, in which *Wuthering Heights* is set. In a dissenting world, Tabby was strict Methodist. While she came as a servant, she was accepted more and more deeply into the family as an essential member. The children could warm their hands on her, and take courage and comfort from her characterful, practical devotion to them. Emily's diary-papers, along with the broad Yorkshire dialect with which Joseph ploughs and harrows up a furrow through the limpid English of *Wuthering Heights*, suggest that Emily found her very funny. In Emily, laughter won acceptance: it admits incongruous and even annoying elements into the company of what is tenable. Joseph ranting in his uncouth, rancorous and mocking Yorkshire; Lockwood making berserk faces at the dogs at the Heights, are both in a strange way welcome. Joseph is like a very peculiar sort of tree which is rooted in that locality and belongs to it, and for Emily Brontë, to be rooted is all. In her Diary Paper for 1834, Emily gave a beautiful sense of what living with Tabby was like, as she described the immediate goings-on in the kitchen:

> Taby said just now Come Anne pilloputate [i.e. pill a potato] Aunt has come into the kitchin just now and said Where are your feet Anne Anne answered On the floor Aunt. Papa opened the parlour door and gave Branwell a letter saying Here Branwell read this and show it to your Aunt and Charlotte. The Gondals are discovering the interior of Gaaldine. Sally Mosley is washing in the back kitchin.
> . . . The kitchin is in a very untidy state Anne and I have not

done our music exercise which consists of *b major* Taby said
on my putting a pen in her face Ya pitter pottering there
instead of pilling a potate. I answered O Dear, O Dear, O
Dear I will derectly With that I get up, take a knife and begin
pilling.

Although this was written nine years later than the period in
which Tabby was first adopted into the household, it records a
situation which clearly had changed little. Anne and Emily still
perceive themselves as children in a world of adult authority
figures, though they are 14 and 16 years old respectively.
Disciplinarians in the form of Aunt, Papa and Tabby keep
erupting through doors to issue requests and recommendations,
to which the 'children' (wrapped in a conspiratorial private
world) return cheeky answers which covertly ridicule the
preoccupations of age (it *is* rather odd to be concerned, they feel,
about the whereabouts of a fellow individual's feet). Aunt
Branwell commands a superficial respect, and despite subsiding
into an obvious fit of smothered giggling, Anne probably does the
decorous thing and stops kneeling up on her chair. Papa, highest
of all in the hierarchy and probably engaged in making an
interesting and significant communication to Branwell—though
the younger children are automatically left out of this serious
matter—is accorded perfect respect. Tabby the servant presents
herself as an authority figure but is really perceived as an equal
and as a marvellous curiosity, of whom the children make outright
but loving fun. Emily takes down everything, just as it happens,
literally and non-committally, trying out a phonetic experiment
to record the rich and cross inflections and idiom of Tabby's testy
speech: 'Ya pitter pottering there instead of pilling a potate'.
Tabby is obviously capable of and practised in the art of the
tirade. Emily has also been rude during the course of writing the
paper, for she has teased Tabby by poking at her face with a pen.
Tabby takes it all in her stride, and eventually does get the
boisterous adolescent to start peeling: she is the nearest of all the
adults to the private game which is the children's innermost
source of excitement and satisfaction. She is loved and mocked,
and intimately accepted in a way that none of the other figures
are—the solitary 'Sally Mosley', an outsider, doing the laundry;
Papa and Aunt making excursions from their sanctums. Being

naughty and getting away with it is seen as a worthwhile pastime: in a larger way, this is all that Catherine and Heathcliff do in *Wuthering Heights*, but their rebellions are uncontained. Love and discipline are absent. Emily's image of the Parsonage kitchen is one of containment; it is a small, safe, enclosed world, highly populated, with its invariable domestic routines overlaid by an exultant stream of emotion and play which records itself in an unpunctuated flow of prose. Simple things, unpretentious utterances, the trivial details of an interior world, are felt as precious and worthy of recording, to be sealed up and kept for the future. The scene is ordinary and commonplace, repeated daily in most homes; the only thing that distinguishes it is the fact that the child's thoughts, perceptions and behaviour have been set down. The telling immortalizes it. The fantasy world which is at the very core of this interior drama, the product of Emily's and Anne's exclusively shared mind, goes on simultaneously and with the same degree of actuality. Tabby moves about in its vicinity; Sally Mosley is standing adjacent to it; but nobody can intrude or occupy it save the two secretive players.

Emily much later told a critical band of schoolgirls in Brussels that she only wished to be 'as God made her', and this fidelity to her own original being was what she prized in Tabby. The relationship implied in the diary-paper is long-standing and enduring. In 1825, Tabby had offered, in ordering them about and seeing to what they needed, the beginnings of a matrix, a substantial presence which could either contain them or against which they could define themselves. One of the most attractive things about Emily is her resolute lack of snobbery, not really humouring Tabby but affirming her as an equal and essential person. When Tabby became old and infirm, and Mr Brontë thought it would be prudent to unburden the household of someone who could no longer be useful as a servant, the children went on hunger-strike until the decision was reversed. Emily took over full responsibility for the invalid, serving the 'servant', nursing her and doing all the household work. It is a measure both of Emily's loyalty—the unwithdrawing quality of her allegiance once it had been given, and her very stern code of moral obligations—and also the success with which she had been grafted to the mothering figure of Tabby. In *Wuthering Heights* the servant Nelly Dean—raised to a higher power by virtue of a modicum of education, and freed of the impenetrable elements of her local dialect, is the matrix of almost the whole book, structuring and colouring it as Tabby had structured and coloured Emily's home.

Tabby also led on to that other home which was the moorland of the world beyond the Parsonage. Emily secured herself in the moors as a source and object of return perhaps more fully than any of her sisters. It may be that the loss of her mother and two elder sisters was partly repaired for her by the dissipation of the mother-archetype both onto the figure of Tabby from whom, because she is finally not blood-kin, a saving detachment might be felt, and on to the impersonal world of nature. A real mother may be prone to disappear; 'mother nature' cannot. In her poems, Emily grew to put her trust in the impersonal; to retard her faith in persons: 'There cast my anchor of Desire/Deep in unknown Eternity'. The earth, for her, contains the grave but is not defined by it. The dead bodies in *Wuthering Heights* are laid in peaty earth which preserves their mortal remains: there seems no final dissolution. When Heathcliff raises the lid of Catherine's coffin he finds that her flesh has not begun to decompose. The dead lie in the earth enclosed and intact. An implicit conception of mother earth shows the underworld where we lay our dead as a system of encapsulating wombs or cells. It is like the past, completely retained in the form of memory—Emily Brontë's art of memory which allows no final reality to any loss.

2 *Visions Rising*

WHEN Patrick Brontë brought home from Leeds a box of twelve wooden soldiers as a gift for Branwell, on the night of 5th June, 1826, he unconsciously unleashed from his children the surge of creativity which would inspire a children's game absorbing to their imaginations throughout their youth; the creation of imaginary worlds (Glasstown, then Angria and Gondal) with their own geography, history, wars and culture; the production of an immense quantity of tiny, hand-made, hand-printed books in which the children wrote their compositions. These books measure around $1^1/_2$ by $2^1/_2$ inches. They are bound with smoothed-out paper-bag covers, and filled with stories and chronicles in minuscule hand-writing. Later, when the authors became more voluminous and their stories more complex in plot and dialogue, the average size of the books trebled. The toy soldiers, who manifested themselves as authors, printers, editors and book-sellers, also undertook journalistic enterprises. Their exploits on the battle-field and in political life (latterly in amorous exploits, especially in Charlotte's Works) were commemorated in poems and lavish illustrations drawn and painted by the children. In the long run, Patrick Brontë's gift may be thought to have resulted—twenty years later—in the publication of *Jane Eyre*, *Wuthering Heights* and *Agnes Grey*. It represented one of those apparently commonplace and unremarkable acts in the life of a group of people which alters the course of their history and releases their identities into new structures and possibilities. Emily at the time of the arrival of the 'Twelves' was nearly 8 years old. She and Charlotte had been at home from Cowan Bridge for a year; in full retreat from the world which had dealt them such an absolute blow, and caused the four remaining children to draw together more intensely, so that the gap made by their losses might appear to close. Emily and Charlotte slept in the same bed, sharing their most private thoughts and preoccupations in the secret 'bed games' which they inaugurated soon after the soldiers made their first appearance. They were tutored by their father, and had the run of his ample personal library as well as access to the Keighley Mechanics' Institute Library.

The gift was delivered to Branwell at the very moment when the children's combined intensities, stimulated by one another's vivid company to the very brim, were ready to break and overflow. From being the victims of destructions which they could not understand, they were now ready to undertake a mutual creation of great power. Charlotte gave an account in her *History of the Year, 1829*, a chronicle of the weighty events in the children's lives, of the exact moment after which, this momentous gift having passed hands from father to son, it was brought into the bedroom shared by Charlotte and Emily:

> next morning Branwell came to our door with a box of soldiers. Emily and I jumped out of bed, and I snatched up one and exclaimed: 'This is the Duke of Wellington! This shall be the Duke!' When I had said this Emily likewise took up one and said it should be hers; when Anne came down, she said one should be hers. Mine was the prettiest of the whole, and the tallest, and the most perfect in every part. Emily's was a grave-looking fellow, and we called him 'Gravey'. Anne's was a queer little thing, much like herself, and we called him 'Waiting-Boy'. Branwell chose his, and called him Buonaparte.

According to Charlotte's account, the girls played fast and loose with their brother's property in taking a fancy to and unceremoniously filching his new and precious toys. His own account is probably nearer the truth: at first, he says, the soldiers were only conceded on loan and later condescendingly handed over. He also names Emily's choice not as 'Gravey' but as 'Parry'—Emily's pseudonym, drawn from the arctic explorer, Captain Edward Parry, who was the little girl's hero, and in whose magnificent person she made her magic appearances in later variations of the game. Possibly the title 'Gravey' was a transitional one, remembered by the scrupulous Charlotte who was fastidious about matters of fact which did not inconvenience the allowable claims of egoism. It seems particularly appropriate that Emily should select a soldier whose rigid facial expression told of a serious and taciturn disposition. Emily herself, whose writing abilities were undeveloped, must have played only an oral part in the game at this early stage. No contributions survive, and no direct account by her of the arrival of the soldiers—unless we consider that in *Wuthering Heights* a parallel or metaphorical account is recorded in the arrival of Heathcliff at the Heights. Chronologically, this is the first major event in the novel, whose consequences are so absolute that without it there could not have been a story. Whereas Mr Brontë went to Leeds and returned with a box of soldiers as a gift for his son, Mr Earnshaw enquires kindly of his little boy, Hindley:

> 'Now, my bonny man, I'm going to Liverpool to-day . . . What shall I bring you? You may choose what you like; only let it be little, for I shall walk there and back; sixty miles each way, that is a long spell.'
> Hindley named a fiddle, and then he asked Miss Cathy; she was hardly six years old, but she could ride any horse in the stable, and she chose a whip.

Whereas Liverpool is said to be 60 miles from the Heights, Leeds is 20 miles from Haworth. Cathy is just under six; Emily had been nearly eight when the extraordinary gift was made. Mr Earnshaw's Yorkshire endearment, 'my bonny man', and his emphasis on the practicalities of his request based on the rigours of a walk that will be 'a long spell', carry touching conviction as a speech of paternal tenderness. The two gifts named are a violin and a whip: art and power, metaphorically. The composite item that Mr Earnshaw does bring home with him in place of the articles on the list is a living being.

It speaks with a kind of 'gibberish that nobody could understand'. It is an urchin with black hair; does not smile, but stares round with a grave expression. This is of course Heathcliff—the changeling, gipsy, cuckoo in the nest, whose presence at the Heights disturbs and violates all the existing relationships in the house. When Nelly says that 'He seemed a sullen, patient child; hardened', it may not be far-fetched to imagine him for a moment as a sort of projection of that small, wooden, inhuman figure, 'Gravey', who was to play Emily's part in the play of Glasstown, and would metamorphose into her male persona, the tremendous 'Parry'. In each case, the gift is not immediately prepossessing. Under cover of a commonplace transaction, something is brought out of one world and introduced into another, with lifelong consequences. The entrance of Branwell's wooden soldiers into Emily's life unleashed first her fantasies, then her art.

Emily's mature art was related to visions, personified, and not always in her control, for they came stealing upon her at certain hours, in the privacy of her bedroom (we remember the inauguration of the 'bed games' with Charlotte), and generally at night. She could not call them up, only be prepared for them, and learned to know by certain signs or 'heralds'—changes of mood, perception and psyche, that they were coming. The moment preceding vision is an 'awful hour'; what she sees arouses but cannot satisfy her, for it 'kills her with desire'. The fantasy world threatens sanity for she must prudently rebel against it in later life: it rules her emotionally, so it is her 'king'. It is personified as male, and forcibly arouses and takes her consciousness; yet the visions are not seen as fundamentally distinct from herself. Like Narcissus, and like Catherine who '*is*' Heathcliff, she reflects her own image in the powerful driving energies of the creative gift, releases and then reabsorbs it. For Emily as for her brother and sisters, the fantasy world which became the world of their art involved not just escape but power, which was one reason why it was so hard to relinquish in favour of everyday reality: through it you could coerce experience. So it was like a whip, and also, because through it experience could be played upon, like Hindley's desired fiddle. Heathcliff in *Wuthering Heights* gratifies these twin demands. He is the essence of her artistic inspiration, providing for us who are without direct autobiographical statements from Emily a veiled insight into what came into the Brontë household in June, 1826, refusing to yield up its mystery and secrecy, letting loose a blast of creative energy which swept on into the entire future. Nothing was the same after the window was opened for this icy, startling wind to enter.

The Glasstown saga would be tedious to relate in detail, as the plots of our childish games do not really bear relating in adult life, not excepting those composed by those of us who are prodigies. It is enough to say that the beginnings of the saga are a mass emigration of the intrepid Twelves from England to Africa in 1770 (everything is precisely dated, though as with most historical writing, authorities do not always concur about the details: Branwell had them embarking in February, Charlotte in March). It was an Africa such as no indigenous African has ever in his wildest dreams imagined. It was inhabited by barbarous Ashantees, a race who had started their wooden existences masquerading as mere ninepins, another gift from their father, but who were terrific fighters and subject to frequent massacre from the invading imperialists on a Napoleonic principle much favoured by Branwell. Each wooden soldier (fading now into the potent personality of his owner) settled in his own colony: Charlotte's Wellingtonsland, Branwell's Sneachiesland, Anne's Ross's land and Emily's Parrysland. Surrounded as they were by hostile nine-pins, it seemed only sensible to combine into the Glasstown Confederacy, which lasted the children through about the next ten years of their lives. After 1832, Charlotte and Branwell founded Angria. The founding of the alternative empire of Gondal by the other twinned pair, Anne and Emily, took place when the latter was around 12 years old, and Charlotte's absence at school at Roe Head interrupted the old game. During earlier stages, the children became kings and queens of the African territories. About a month after their first landing, the Twelves also discovered that there were mighty presences in Africa not previously catalogued in the travel-writings of explorers who had penetrated the Dark Continent. These were the Genii, the towering Beings into whose terrifying but benign shape (for they acted as guardians of their chosen soldiers) the children who master-minded the game had swollen: Tallii, Emmii, Annii and Brannii, whose awesome powers were supernatural and who could take up the astonished Twelves in the palm of one hand.

Charlotte's water-colour of *The Bay of Glasstown* shows very clearly the influence of John Martin, the romantic painter of exotic monumental architecture and landscapes, either undergoing or about to undergo some titanic convulsion or conflagration. Towering columns of a vaguely Egyptian or Babylonian species reach up grandly to a level with the vista of a mountain range in the background: the whole picture is tinted with a sky-blue wash, as if to dramatize the theme of aspiration and its grandeur which held the children's imaginations. Upon one tower are perched two angelic-looking figures, one with wings, which might perhaps be a pair of presiding Genii majestically surveying the world. Charlotte's Glasstown celebrates a power that is gorgeous and unearthly, risky, dangerous and Satanic. Milton and Byron, embodying the conception of evil as energy, inform Charlotte's vision. Parrysland was nothing like this. 'Gravey', that jaundiced, satiric and realistic individual, had built, as Emily was to build *Wuthering*

Heights, on the solid earth. Emily's Africa, according to
Charlotte's account of 'A Day at Parry's Palace', was like
Haworth on a particularly bad day:

> I was immediately struck with the changed aspect of
> things; all the houses were ranged in formal rows they
> contained four rooms each with a little garden in front. No
> proud castle or splendid palace towered insultingly over the
> cottages around. No high-born noble claimed allegiance of
> his vassals or swayed his broad lands with hereditary pride,
> and every inch of ground was inclosed with stone walls. . . .
> Nasty factories with their tall black chimneys breathing thick
> columns of almost tangible smoke discoloured not that sky of
> dull hazy hue. . . . Parry's palace was a square building
> surmounted by blue slates and some round stone pumpkins.
> . . . And the convenient offices such as wash-house, back-
> kitchen stable and coal-house were built in a line and backed
> by a row of trees.

Lord Charles Wellesley, Charlotte's persona, is mildly amused by
this unbendingly introverted literality. Had Parry no sense of
caste and the fitness of things (he sits at dinner in stony silence
taking no notice of his dandy-guests, though Wellesley feels sure
he has never set eyes on such refined persons before)? It seems that
Parry's notion of architectural ornament only extends to the
oddity of a stone pumpkin or two, and that his uncouth world has
no class system. It is a working world, which has an industrial
system, and is mindful of the laundry. Emily's fantasy is shown as
having tenacious roots in life as it is, rather than the hazy blue
world of Charlotte's imaginings. Parrysland is no distance at all
from the Parsonage kitchen of Emily's Diary-paper.

Charlotte's account of Parrysland ends with Ross (Anne) being
taken ill from over-eating; and, Death being imminent, the
apparition of the *Genius Emily* who 'cured with an incantation and
vanished'. This device of 'making alive again' was essential to the
continuation of the cycle, not just because the characters were
liable to collapse from over-eating, but more seriously because
Branwell's tastes inclined to the bloodthirsty. He favoured
wholesale massacres running with blood, dismemberings and
cannibalisms which threatened by butchering the entire caste to
terminate the play on many occasions. Branwell's unwholesome

relish for bloodbaths had to be tolerated not only because the meaning of the game lay in the mutual participation of the whole family but also because of the licence given in the game to the unrestricted imagination. There had to be both closeness and freedom. If it came into a player's head to have carnage, then carnage had to happen, according to the rigid law of fantasy. Branwell, as an only boy, was inclined to take his role as the unique 'King' amongst a hareem of inferior 'Queens' with superciliousness, and to indulge his pugilistic tastes (later, he learned to box with the local youths). The logical end must be the abandonment of the game. But nobody, including that small, red-haired conqueror, actually wanted this to happen. They had worked their identities in with those of the heroes into whom they had breathed their life, and whose adventures were their adventures. It may also have been intrinsic to the girls' preferences to place creation before destruction. Though their military exploits could be just as violent; their heroes full of the virile and militaristic qualities, and themselves not disinclined to bloody revolution, Charlotte, Emily and Anne saw the downhill tendency of such unmitigated ferocity. They invented the device of 'making alive again' as a way of resurrecting the dead. The Chief Geniuses who were the four children would, in the event of an adventure proving terminal for one of the wooden men, graciously enter themselves on to the field of slaughter and by a mysterious art revitalize the stricken warriors, who could then continue the game. This technique of 'making alive again' is not unusual or interestingly precocious among children's games: most children discover it for themselves. But perhaps it has the status of a hint in the context of the predicament of a child of 8 like Emily, who has to adapt to a triple bereavement and feelings of dread associated with the outside world, and find some way of asserting that she can outlive these deaths; that, for her inner self, they have no final reality to which her future need be subdued. The children in 'making alive again' say that they have power and control, where in fact they are most weak. In Emily Brontë's novel, characters are experienced by the reader as continuing energies and presences after their deaths. As the child Catherine taps on the window in Lockwood's dream, so the dead, stabilized in a past form, at a certain age, beat upon the consciousness of the living. Heathcliff sees Catherine encased in her grave, years on, exactly

as she was, waiting for him to join her. I think that the secrets
Emily learned from childhood play, and inscribed on her memory
and in her stories, were maintained over the years into adult life as
a private resource. She tried out the art of 'making alive again' in
Wuthering Heights against the mortal processes of the natural
world, seeing how far that art may credibly be sustained against
the resistant medium of time, change and mortality.

Glasstown, and later Gondal, then, embodied myths of power.
They represented a private reality as incomprehensible to anyone
not involved as Heathcliff in his advent at Wuthering Heights,
who was rejected by the family. The Brontë children's game
involved not only heroic fantasies but brawls between the players
in their personae as Chief Genii. Tabby thought the children, in
their fits of incomprehensible violence, were plain mad. She
departed at speed on one occasion for the sanctuary of the
normality of her nephew's cottage, breathlessly declaring:

> Willum! Ya mun gooa up to Mr Bontë's, for aw'm sure yon
> childer's all goan mad, and aw darn't stop i' the house ony
> longer wi'en, an' aw'll stay till woll ya come back.

The highly wrought children burst into a 'great crack o'laughin' '
when William appeared on this errand. Tabby was not wrong to
feel that the dedicated intensity of their game was abnormal and
out of control, for they invested in it frantic excitements which
were hard to give up later in favour of the undramatic realities of
impoverished lives, fighting for a modest independence as
governesses in other peoples' houses, and teaching school-
children who did not want to learn. Fantasy was a drug to which
Charlotte would have loved to keep up her addiction. Branwell's
Bonaparte-role with which he most fatally identified himself
utterly unfitted him for making a living as a painter, or a railway
clerk, or a tutor, or anything else which society had to offer him:
fantasy gave place to alcohol and drug-abuse, and he was dead at
31 years old. Tabby's conclusion that 'yon childer's all goan mad'
was not true, but dangers were there from the beginning. Aunt
Branwell and Patrick Brontë, sitting apart and secluded in their
respective privacies, must have heard the row at a muffled
distance, Aunt no doubt disapprovingly. Their father
remembered being called upon to settle disputes between
Bonaparte, Hannibal, Caesar and the Iron Duke, which he must

have undertaken according to his usual conscientious principles of strict reason. Aunt Branwell perhaps endeavoured to quell childish buoyancy by the application of depressing texts stressing the ghastliness of mortality; that we are born to die; that we cannot predict our hour of departure; that suffering is our earthly lot. On Aunt's teapot was the invigorating motto: 'To me to live is Christ/To die is gain'. Vast sewing-sessions calculated to flatten the imagination and imbue the young soul with fortifying boredom were also used to regulate the Brontë daughters into a more 'feminine' cast of mind.

Emily's distaste for the 'ladylike', and therefore for every facet of woman's existence which the nineteenth-century thought of as obligatory began from the earliest days. Her immense physical courage and fortitude alone would have unfitted her for such a pusillanimous ideal. In every way that mattered, she took a 'male' part, and later adapted that role quite naturally to the women of the world of Gondal, her poetry and fiction. In an early game, Emily took the part of Charles II in a dramatic reliving on Oak Apple Day of his hiding-out in the boughs of an oak-tree at Worcester from the Cromwellian soldiers. No oak being to hand, she climbed her father's cherry-tree by his window, in order to represent this heroic role, broke a branch and came crashing down to the ground. The idea of Emily as a 'king' of her fantasy world is apt (she was always a Royalist by inclination, and re-enacted the Civil Wars of England and France in the Royalist-republican conflicts of the Gondal saga); so is her climbing. She aspired, and seemed built without a touch of common physical fear. In another age, with a hint of disapproval combined with a patronizing assurance that she would grow out of it in due time, she would have been called a 'tom-boy'. Emily never did grow out of it. That is to say, she never lost her nerve. As a young woman she is said to have beaten her beloved dog, Keeper, with her bare hands on his face for refusing to be house-trained, till she drew blood, and he submitted. On another occasion, John Greenwood, the Haworth stationer, wrote in his diary of a dog-fight between Keeper and another village dog:

She never spoke a word, nor appeared the least at a loss what to do, but rushed at once into the kitchen, took the pepper box, and away into the lane, where she found the two savage brutes each holding the other by the throat, in deadly grip, while several other animals, who thought themselves men, were standing looking on like cowards as they were, afraid to touch them—there they stood gaping, watching this fragile creature spring upon the beasts—seizing Keeper round the neck with one arm, while with the other hand she dredges well their noses with pepper, and separating them by force of her great will, driving Keeper, that great powerful dog, before her into the house, never once noticing the men, so called, standing there thunderstruck at the deed.

This is the behaviour of Emily Brontë as a mature woman in her mid-twenties. The tomboyishness so disparaged by lovers of effete behaviour in women has not been outlived but rather encouraged and strengthened. Only a social fear stronger than her commitment to physical and mental hardihood, allowing inroads to be made by social conventions as to what is and is not 'proper' to young ladies, could have weakened this personal courage. Emily was wonderfully impervious to social pressure of this brain-softening sort and did not allow her will to be sapped by it. The gesture of personal weakness, noticed earlier, in her clinging to Charlotte's arm in the Brussels school-yard may be seen in this context as a way of defending not a timid, vulnerable soul but 'no coward soul' who fears to yield to that insidious spinelessness with which female society had the subversive power to break the back of genuine originality. When she was bitten by a dog which she took to be rabid, Emily instantly went indoors and mutely cauterized the wound with red-hot tongs. She made no allowance for herself: silent courage was a reflex action bred of long schooling of her will. Emily's drawings of her dogs, Grasper and Keeper, and the picture which is supposed to be of her Merlin hawk, Hero, his eyes, beak and talons as sharply etched as in an engraving, show her deep affinity with the silent, self-contained and instinctual power of the animal world. Her reserve and taciturnity guarded a comparable pride and self-containment from the chattering of a social world. In her diary-papers, constant reference is made to her animals, a growing population, much to Aunt Branwell's horror, for who would wish to live in the barbarous north surrounded by a zoo of pigeons, pheasants, 'Victoria and Adelaide (geese) . . . ensconced in the peat-house(.)

Keeper . . . in the kitchen—Hero in his cage' (as Emily recorded in 1841), together with miscellaneous cats and dogs and the abiding menace of the probability of new acquisitions? One of the curiosities of *Wuthering Heights* is the abundance of named canine life, and its active contribution to events. Whereas other Romantic poets had stopped short in their devotion to nature at its harmlessly vegetable or rocky effects, such as Wordsworth's 'rocks and stones and trees', Emily was, from her earliest days, devoted to nature seen in a more fully realistic perspective, including its predatory and carnivorous elements. She moves sharply on from Wordsworth and Coleridge and that bare landscape which entertains animal life only in the form of sheep and sheep-dogs, and which loves this bloodless nature as a benign 'mother', toward the Darwinian revolution and a conception of the survival of the fittest. Yet she can still identify this larger nature, with its bloodshed, as her home. Her nature—from its earliest childhood—had included the unacceptably ferocious as it vigorously denied the constructions of the amiably ladylike.

Emily and Charlotte remained both physically and imaginatively close until 1831, when Emily was 12 years old, sharing a bed and continuing with those under-cover Bed Plays which, as Charlotte wrote enigmatically, 'mean secret plays . . . very nice ones . . . very strange ones'. They appear to have concerned the incarceration of mutinous aristocratic children in the dungeons of the Palace of Instruction on a fictitious island. The allegory is not very difficult to decipher, considering Aunt's autocratic rule of law in the Parsonage. They read *Blackwood's*, and Byron, and Scott. But in 1831, Charlotte having been sent off to school at Roe Head, Emily's partnership with her new and lasting twin, Anne, was established, and with it came the founding of their kingdom of Gondal. Ellen Nussey later spoke of Anne and Emily as walking out together on the moors with their arms 'twined' round one another's waists; 'like twins, inseparable companions in the very closest sympathy, which never had any interruption'. It must have been a relief for Anne to have a chance of escaping the reign of terror in Aunt's Calvinistic bed for the fresh air of Emily's fantasy world. She was smaller, milder, gentler, and more traditionally pious than Emily. To Charlotte she was always the baby of the family, 'dear gentle Anne', to be taken under a protective wing. Despite Anne's real and crippling timidity, I imagine that many other Victorian families would have found her rather worryingly unconventional and free-thinking. But where all minds are spirited and strong-willed, the least obviously assertive must necessarily seem to exemplify softness. Anne could not have twinned herself as firmly to the granite Emily if she had really been such a tender plant: in her novels, she was to protest about nearly everything she encountered in the outside world, from the injustice of its marriage laws to the wickedness of the 'Christian' doctrine of damnation. Anne and Emily drew so close that they shared one another's being.

In Charlotte's absence, they founded Gondal. Emily retained the idea of a fictitious island from the bed-play, as well as the palace, dungeons, civil wars, and royal princes and princesses in exile. Gondal was an island in the North Pacific; Gaaldine another in the South Pacific; the former a northern and the latter being a tropical landscape. There must have been detailed maps, and prose accounts, but these have been lost or destroyed. We know tantalizingly little of the Gondal saga except what has been painstakingly pieced together from Anne's and Emily's poetry (the latter copied 'Gondal Poems' into a note-book of their own); from lists of Gondal names jotted down by Anne for her own reference; and from the scraps of information in the diary-papers. What has been deduced is either minimal or highly speculative, for the longitudes and latitudes of their secret world have gone down into the grave with the imaginations which devised them. This is as it was intended to be. The diary notes reveal fragmentary news, obviously as immediate to the joint authors as the current affairs gleaned from the *Leeds Intelligencer*, or possibly more so. In 1834, Emily records that 'The Gondals are discovering the interior of Gaaldine'; in 1841 on her 23rd birthday, Emily records 'wild rainy weather'; goes through the household's events and projects, concluding:

> The *Gondalians* are at present in a threatening state, but there is no open rupture as yet. All the princes and princesses of the Royalty are at the Palace of Instruction. I have a good many books on hand, but I am sorry to say that as usual I make small progress with any. However, I have just made a new regularity paper! and I mean *verb sap* to do great things. And now I must close, sending from far an exhortation,

'Courage, courage,' to exiled and harassed Anne, wishing she
was here.

We can see from this last remark the fact that the world of Gondal
was not a sealed world bare of relationship to the facts of their life.
The exiled princes and princesses of the inner life of Gondal have
their replicas in reality in the form of 'exiled and harassed Anne',
hating her position as governess in Scarborough and needing to
draw upon that virtue so prized by the characters in Gondal,
'Courage, courage', in order to survive from day to day in a
loveless treadmill routine in a stranger's house. The state of
continuous crisis which seems to have been the political climate of
revolutionary Gondal keeps the fantasy alive with suspense. It is a
huge enterprise, as multitudinous as life itself, in which the author
has 'a good many books on hand' rather than a single, linear
narrative. In a parallel paper, Anne mentions that she is 'now
engaged in writing the fourth volume of *Solala Vernon's Life*'.
Gondal teems with possibilities. It has large and multiplying
numbers of characters; numerous Kingdoms and plenty of
unexplored territory. Four years later, Emily opens her 1841
paper, and records that she and Anne have been on their first long
journey, to York, staying overnight, and then back via Keighley,
'walking home on Wednesday morning'. The wonders of York are
not described at all. The Gondals had been taken with them, and
their adventures form the material for the note:

> And during our excursion we were, Ronald Macalgin, Henry
> Angora, Juliet Augusteena, Rosabella Esmalden, Ellen and
> Julian Egremont, Catherine Navarre, and Cordelia
> Fitzaphnold, escaping from the palaces of instruction to join
> the Royalists who are hard driven at present by the
> victorious Republicans. The Gondals still flourish bright as
> ever. I am at present writing a work on the First Wars. . . .
> We intend sticking by the rascals as long as they delight us,
> which I am glad to say they do at present.

Anne's note sounds weary, as though she feels that the *Gondal
Chronicles* might be getting out of hand, and that the time might
shortly be coming when it will be right to put away childish things:

> The Gondals are at present in a sad state. The Republicans
> are uppermost, but the Royalists are not quite overcome. The

young sovereigns, with their brothers and sisters, are still at the Palace of Instruction. The Unique Society, about half a year ago, were wrecked on a desert island as they were returning from Gaul. They are still there, but we have not played at them much yet. The Gondals in general are not in first-rate playing condition. Will they improve?

The note of unadulterated wretchedness in Anne's diary-paper reflects not only the fact that the endlessly unfolding cycle of Gondal, with the tendency of the mother plant to send out green shoots in all directions which must then be followed up (the Unique Society's shipwreck), was beginning to loom as an uncontrollable labour rather than a spontaneous joy, but also her dark experiences of Branwell's liaison with their employer, Mrs Robinson, at Scarborough, his addiction and degradation at home. Emily's paper is grimly positive. She sticks loyally by the 'rascals' in the fantasy, faithfully recording the names of the heroes they impersonated on the long walk home from Keighley and determinedly keeping those jewels of her imagination which no external suffering can dim 'bright as ever'. It is not that she has abandoned the real world for the inner, for her aside referring, one supposes, to Branwell is harsh and caustic, 'merely desiring that everybody could be as comfortable as myself and as undesponding, and then we should have a very tolerable world of it'. Anne had been in exile, and forced to live continuously with her face up against the realities of Branwell's liaison: it was hard for her to find compensation in the Gondal fantasy as Emily, with her ruthless dedication to the inner life, could, so as to find the game 'bright as ever'. Yet her comments on Emily's books and work in this diary-paper show that she took a joy in Emily herself that was deep and positive, and that it was worth keeping the Gondals active on account of that love. Emily's reaction to Branwell's affliction (he was now at home destroying the family life by his vagaries and sufferings) was the practical one of doing all she could to help her father cope, and the slightly less useful one of living out the conviction that suffering is really a matter of will-power, and not understanding that her own case might be unique. It is hard not to feel that in applying her personal standards to other people who were not fitted to live up to them, Emily might have done them less than justice. She lived out, as her Gondal characters did, an uncompromising commitment to her personal code, and perhaps made little allowance for the fact that few persons have the facilities to create a Gondal within themselves in which to rest and derive the power to be 'as undesponding' as herself.

The founding of Gondal by the 12–13 year-old Emily represented an absolute covering of her losses, together with a durable place for her expanding spirit to inhabit, since it lasted out the remaining 17 years of her life-span. Two of the important ingredients which allowed this to happen were, I think, the female character of the Gondal empire, and the closeness of its landscape to the moors which were the setting of her own deepest spiritual affinities. The 1845 diary paper had said that 'we were' three male and five female characters on the walk from Keighley to Haworth, and this bias toward the female was one of the most significant aspects of the world of Gondal, singling it out from the bellicose masculinities of Glasstown. This is not to say that Gondal was a tame or peaceful place: on the contrary, complex and full-scale wars requiring assiduous commentary raged unabated, and individuals were employed in doing the normal thing in wartime (and little else), betraying one another, turning coats, ambushing, seducing, rebelling, quelling and digging graves for one another on a full-time basis. They were definitely a nasty species, women just as much as men. Emily and Anne did not really judge them for these activities: they liked black-haired young men with Byronic temperaments, 'basilisk eyes' and amoral instincts, and they were not averse to the revenge ethic, so at variance with the duty of Christian forgiveness:

> Compassion reigns a little while,
> Revenge eternally.

However, as historians of the fantasy world, they did not really feel called upon to give judgment; as the poets of the saga, they were mouthpieces, through which the characters could speak. But Gondal was a place of female power where patriarchy (despite frequent incarcerations of princesses) was not admired as it was in Branwell's Glasstown. There were dashing heroes and unscrupulous tyrants like the Emperor Julius Brenzaida in Emily's grim and authentic ballad:

> King Julius left the south country
> His banners all bravely flying;
> His followers went out with Jubilee
> But they shall return with sighing.

Emily was the only one of the sisters ever to tune the ballad form to its original rough, stressful anonymity, catching the tense fatalism and irony which are intrinsic to the form. Julius's conquests seem to have formed a significant element in the plot, and Gondal, like Glasstown and Angria, ran with blood from end to end, but Emily outlived the war-mania which gripped them all as children when they had not come to reflect upon the realities of war:

> Why ask to know what date, what clime?
> There dwelt our own humanity,
> Power-worshippers from earliest time,
> Foot-kissers of triumphant crime
> Crushers of helpless misery,
> Crushing down Justice, honouring Wrong . . .

> Our corn was garnered months before,
> Threshed out and kneaded up with gore;
> Ground when the ears were milky sweet
> With furious toil of hoofs and feet . . .

This is the last poem Emily is known to have written, a final statement in the Gondal epic which had itself fed on war for its plot, yet now records the product of war as a sickening kind of bread made up of a dough moistened with blood rather than water. Gondal had led Emily on a journey right through its interior and out the other side. From a vague feeling of stimulation at the idea of war, she moved morally toward its true implications, and a setting of 'corn' (the female and creative) against 'blood' (the male and destructive). The goodness in the ears of corn is 'milky sweet', but man's threshing of his harvest takes the form of a mindless act of violence. The milk of human kindness—or mother's milk—is wasted, and in 'helpless misery' the victims of war are spiritually and physically famished. In common usage, the word 'humanity' carried a positive connotation, but Emily's view of 'our own humanity' (she too is implicated) is angry and disgusted.

In the saga, Julius with his talent for shedding blood and inspiring others to do so seems to have been less important than

Augusta Almeda and Rosina Alcona. Fifteen years after his death, Rosina meditates on his grave with a conviction of his reality comparable to that of Heathcliff's absorption in Catherine 18 years after her death. This is the most famous poem of the whole Gondal cycle, spoken in a powerful female voice stating an austerely passionate dedication to its deepest affinity:

> Cold in the earth, and the deep snow piled above thee!
> Far, far removed, cold in the dreary grave!
> Have I forgot, my Only Love, to love thee,
> Severed at last by Time's all-wearing wave? . . .
>
> Cold in the earth, and fifteen wild Decembers
> From those brown hills have melted into spring—
> Faithful indeed is the spirit that remembers
> After such years of change and suffering!

The elegiac voice, rather than the noise of military or political encounters, characterizes the Gondal world. Emily was rather partial to writing dirges, and specialized in them for her Gondal poems: yet the elegy in her hands is vigorous and affirmative in stressing the value and power of human love against the forces that threaten to erode or absorb it. The 'deep snow' of many winters buries the grave itself, but the personality that is coldly unreachable at two removes from the living, beneath drifting snow on the crust of earth, is defiantly insisted on as an enduringly real identity. This is a recreative voice. 'The spirit that remembers' is drawing on Emily Brontë's art of memory to reclaim the losses that cannot logically be reversed. Gondal, seen in terms of this female power of creativity, leads into the 'real' world in an effort to bond back that condition of being 'far removed' and 'changed', the severing which is the mortal condition and a theme of all Emily's work. Equally, we can see that Gondal led out of the Parsonage and up onto the moors, that other substantial home of Emily's imagination—embellished with the lochs, estuaries and mountains of a Scotland which, though she could never personally visit it, she had read of in Scott and James Hogg and absorbed as a place where she could belong and grow. The earth in this poem is not an enemy. The 'brown hills' contain the grave but echo the plain forms of a landscape that is loved for its sombreness and individuality. Julius' heart is covered by 'heath and fern-leaves', unembellished by any adjectives, for they are things of such inconceivable beauty in themselves to Emily Brontë that she feels (and makes us feel) that they provide a natural and protective covering for his resting-place. Gondal therefore intersects with reality by taking root in the moorland that was literally outside Emily's window; the 'world within' looks out onto a mirroring outer reality.

When we speak of someone as being 'self-contained' (as Emily is often called) we really mean that she can afford to be: she is nourished by a feeling of exceptional safety and security. Emily's principle of inward safety, which could only operate when the eyes were off her, but then was absolute, was provided by Gondal. Its large and interesting population made solitude teem with life. 'Emily is in the parlour, brushing the carpet', recorded Charlotte in 1829; the inner world would drain household chores of boredom. The large spaces of the natural world, every configuration of the moors, would be as familiar as first cousins, because of this inner safety. She could suffer with what appears to us as superhuman stoicism because of the conception which she had lived out through her life that pain is merely a sensation within one, over which it is possible to assert power and control. Emily found from an early age that the greatest good is to have one's being within, and to defend it from any intrusion.

3 Why I Did Cast the World Away

IN 1835, on the eve of Emily's 17th birthday, the Eden of the shared inner world was broken by a full-scale expulsion and scattering of the young people. Branwell was sent to seek admission to the Royal Academy to train as an artist; Charlotte was offered the position of teacher at Roe Head, and Emily was to accompany her as a pupil. Patrick Brontë intended, he said, to keep 'my dear little Anne' at home with him for another year. The imperative thing was that all his children should be fitted to support themselves in the event of their father's death, which would leave them literally destitute, without a roof over their heads, and in any event they must be able to contribute as adults to the upkeep of the household. Each was acutely aware of the urgency of this need, and though his daughters whole-heartedly detested the idea of the only career which would be open to them as respectable middle-class young women (as governess or teacher), they were dedicated to gaining the means of independence. Only Branwell with the advantage of his gender, but the disadvantage of its heavy onus loaded onto his impressionable and highly-strung nature, could expect to undertake a trade he might be supposed to enjoy. The only 'stranger' with whom Emily had been in previous contact—since the tragedies wrought by 'strangers' at Cowan Bridge—was Charlotte's extremely harmless friend, Ellen Nussey, who had stayed at the Parsonage in 1833: she had inspired Emily with a minimum of fright and no hostility, but then she had got remarkably little out of Emily either, who 'did not often look at you: she was too reserved. . . . She talked very little'. At home Emily went her own way and did not make concessions.

In 1835 she was sent out into an institution in which she felt herself to be an outcast and a misfit. Whereas on the moors at home she could stride around whistling to her dog in a way that to her was natural but to others would seem 'mannish', and within limits that she understood could do whatever came into her head, now she was put out into the society of the 'ladylike', where you must not have genius but only accomplishments; you were not

allowed to keep quiet if you had nothing to say but required to
enter into a twittering conversation more proper to an aviary than
to a society of rational creatures; you had to learn a little of this
and a smattering of that; train yourself to walk as if, instead of a
solid pair of legs, you ran on casters; and be regimented into a set
routine from which there was no deviation. This is not to say that
the school run by the four Miss Woolers was anything out of the
ordinary. On the contrary, it was perfectly normal, fairly rational
and certainly benign, with nothing like the austerities of Cowan
Bridge. Emily simply could not bear such normality, for she had
not learned to define herself according to socially acceptable
categories of what is 'male' and 'female', allowed or disallowed.
She had wanted to judge and be judged as people were in Gondal,
by the essential, ungendered 'soul', rather than by the
superficialities of clothes or hairstyle: by that aspect of our being
which is not expressed in outer garments. Her sense of offence was
shared and expressed in her journal by Charlotte: 'If those girls
knew how I loathed their company they would not seek mine so
much as they do. . . . I crept up to the bed-room to be alone for the
first time that day'. They missed being alone, with the peace to
dream, and the freedom of the moors. Emily could not eat, and
became ill with a home-sickness so desperate that Charlotte
thought she would die of it and 'obtained her recall'. Branwell also
came home, a miserable and inexplicable failure. In a sense, his
position was the converse of Emily's. He was expected to get on
with the business of being a man. Yet in London he felt so
dwarfed, confused and inadequate that he could not bring himself
to sidle in through the doors of the Academy, wandered round the
city, got drunk and came home to Haworth. Emily's life included
two further excursions into the outside world, in 1837 as a
governess at Law Hill, Halifax, and in 1842 studying in Belgium.
Each time, she hastened home and crouched there recovering.
The real story of her adult life is therefore not so much in its
external events as in the uneventful existence in Haworth. In her
poem beginning 'O thy bright eyes must answer now', Emily asks
her visionary gift to plead her case as counsel for the defence in the
trial to which the outside world and its standards puts her:

> Stern Reason is to judgement come
> Arrayed in all her forms of gloom:

Wilt thou my advocate be dumb?
No, radiant angel, speak and say
Why I did cast the world away;

Why I have persevered to shun
The common paths that others run;
And on a strange road journeyed on
Heedless alike of Wealth and Power—
Of Glory's wreath and Pleasure's flower.

Though she defines her relinquishing of the outside world as a positive choice rather than a negative retreat from the unbearable, the image of the trial-scene in which she must give her reasons for 'casting the world away' shows that she was open to a sense of failure, and to the charge of being irrational or unstable.

More deeply, she felt that any insanity was on the other side. She had moved out into a world where they insisted on judging you by the maddest standards, such as the length of your hair, the curvature of your skirt or the measurements of your sleeves. No genuinely sane person, Emily felt, could either approve or even understand such criteria. When she went away, to Roe Head, Halifax and Brussels, she felt stranded in a world of agreed and communal insanity, in which she must guard and defend her singularity with her life. She was clearly perplexed by her 'clothed' image. Mrs Gaskell, not herself exactly radical in these matters (as we see by the retained 'Mrs' which insists on a social label for an 'authoress' rather than an author) seemed to think Emily must have looked rather a fright in the old-fashioned outfit which she wore in Brussels:

> Emily had taken a fancy to the fashion, ugly and preposterous even during its reign, of gigot sleeves, and persisted in wearing them long after they were 'gone out'. Her petticoats, too, had not a curve or wave in them, but hung straight and long, clinging to her lank figure.

Mrs Gaskell, mother of four nice girls, not one of whom would have allowed herself to be seen in anything but the prettiest sleeves, the 'curviest' and 'waviest' petticoats, allowed herself to betray a tone of incredulity to think that a girl born disadvantaged with a 'lank' figure should not disguise it in billowing rotundities of cloth. She cannot sympathize with a person who is far too proud to be vain. I do not think that Emily Brontë, who had 'been' all the characters in the Gondal myth, both male and female, and who was to assert in *Wuthering Heights* that Catherine 'is' Heathcliff, sharing a soul, considered that any stereotypical difference between the sexes should be maintained. She seemed to classify according to the genes you inherit and the conditioning you receive rather than the gender into which, as if by accident, your soul falls; though there is also a deep association of the female with fruitfulness and rebirth in her works. Assuming this, but forced to go out into a world where such self-evident truths were considered not only as peculiarities but also as wickedness by persons dedicated from birth to the pursuit of the 'ladylike', based on an unquestioned assumption that women were natural and negative opposites to men, Emily must have felt that, if she opened her mouth to declare herself, she must appear (like the child Heathcliff in his uncouth entrance into the Heights) to be uttering 'gibberish that nobody could understand'. They would think her as mad as she thought them. She is recorded as a silence in the outside world.

Emily's male pseudonym, Ellis Bell, under which she published her poetry and novel, was an appropriate way for her to offer herself as an author, in her own person, rather than as a woman angrily failing to be what she did not want to be anyway, in the world's judging eyes. It is a neutral, simple, rather dignified and down-to-earth name. It expresses, as do Currer for Charlotte and Acton for Anne, the shared antagonism to false gentility which positively reinforced the family's shyness, soliciting a fair hearing from a public to whom 'poetess' was a euphemism for 'poetaster', and to be an 'authoress' was to announce yourself as consciously second-rate. In *Wuthering Heights* Emily showed the power of conditioning and faulty education to distort and degrade. She discerned the effects of an education which was designed to encourage a certain sort of feebleness in the children at Roe Head and in Brussels, and (having no natural gift for patience and no intention of cultivating it) despised them. She was not joking when she told the Law Hill school-children whom she was trying to teach that the only creature she could actually bring herself to like in the place was the house-dog. Dogs never dress up; are not affected; are generally of sound instinct. Mary Taylor, Charlotte's outspoken friend, recognized as most people must have, the anger which Emily in her role as misfit harboured against the tyranny of the fatuous and frivolous in social affairs. In 1843, she wrote to Ellen Nussey:

> Tell me something about Emily Brontë. I can't imagine how the newly acquired qualities can *fit in*, in the same head and heart that is occupied with the old ones. Imagine Emily turning over prints or 'taking wine' with any stupid fop and preserving her temper and politeness.

This was four years before Emily enlightened the world, by presenting it with Lockwood in *Wuthering Heights*, as to her opinion of 'any stupid fop'. Mary Taylor testifies that Emily's behaviour inclined toward rudeness, even by her own standards which stressed frankness before courtesy. Being agreeable would not be seen as a moral imperative, candour being preferred to kindliness. Where her sister Charlotte's supply of small-talk was impoverished and halting, Emily's was non-existent. She brought doom and blight to any social situation to which she was invited, sitting not monosyllabically but in total silence throughout. One would not wish her as a guest upon one's worst enemy. There is even the disconcerting possibility that Emily was capable, with one part of her being, of enjoying the torment of her host and fellow guests. In presenting the sociable Lockwood's squirming efforts to get his bearings in the rude 'misanthropist's Heaven' of the Heights, by ingratiating himself according to an imported unctuous code of manners, she demonstrates with humour of a wickedly knowing sort a perfect awareness of the embarrassing effects of taciturnity on someone eager to make contact. There is a sort of vengeance in putting the social world at the mercy of the anti-social, with the polite Lockwood committing every kind of social gaffe. Emily must have both initiated and sarcastically observed plenty of social unease directly caused by her own behaviour. She could not even conceive of being a Lockwood: to her he appears mad. Even the dogs think so at Wuthering Heights, and go for him accordingly. She 'cast the world aside' because she recognized that it operated with different organs of vision to her own, seeing different shapes and colours, from a different perspective and according to a foreign ethic.

Emily settled deeply back into the routines of the Parsonage, keeping company with Branwell for the next two years, studying music and German, and writing her personal poetry. Her frequent accusations against herself to the effect that she is more 'terrifically and idiotically and brutally STUPID' than ever, afflicted with pernicious laziness, are probably to be taken with a pinch of salt, the perfectionist's inevitable falling-short. In the winter of 1836–7, Charlotte wrote to Robert Southey and Branwell to Wordsworth and to *Blackwood's Magazine* on the possibilities of their becoming professional writers. Southey was benevolently discouraging on the grounds of Charlotte's unfortunate membership of the wrong sex; Wordsworth did not answer, taking exception to the idiotic and arrogant tone with which his disciple petitioned this elderly Olympian deity. Emily took no part in this brave effort to reach out of obscurity into the public world. She nursed Tabby, who was lame, and got on with her work. She was later described by tradesmen as kneading dough on the kitchen table, with a book propped in front of her, surrounded by odds and ends of paper on which she must have been writing down fragments of Gondal and nature-poems as they occurred to her. It is an image of an enclosed and busy state of peace. This is borne out by the Diary Paper of 1837 which records the whereabouts and occupations of the other members of the family and the Gondal people ('Charlotte working in Aunt's room . . . Anne and I writing in the drawing-room . . . Zamorna at Eversham'), including the lovely phrase for happiness which typifies Emily's lack of limpness in response; her feeling that real pleasure is something strenuous, energetic and essentially ordered: 'All tight and right in which condition it is to be hoped we shall all be this day 4 years'. She records their ages as they will be then, typically down to a mathematically precious fraction of a month in her own case, 'myself 22 and 10 months and a peice', with its pleasant mingling of a touch of pedantry and a dash of bad spelling. She ends with a scrap of conversation snatched from the air:

> Aunt: Come Emily its past 4 o'clock
> Emily: Yes, Aunt   Exit Aunt
> Ann: Well, do you intend to write in the evening
> Emily: Well, what think you

This is quite pointless yet totally fascinating. Like their mother's faded letters which Patrick would draw out of the reserves of time to show to Charlotte, and like the glimpses of Catherine's journal in *Wuthering Heights,* Emily decides to scoop up a few idle or functional words from where they have been dropped, and keep them secretly for the future. It is a joke. against Aunt to immortalize her petty intrusion; an affirmation of the fun of the subversive freedom mutually enjoyed with Anne. Emily at this time was coming into her own, for the tiny old nursery where the children had played their first games was now recognized as her own private room, with her camp-bed across the window for dreaming on, and a low chair for sitting to write.

Yet later that year (though the date is uncertain) Emily was again out of her sanctuary, teaching at Law Hill, Halifax, a large dark-stone building run by a Miss Patchett, where they took 40 girls. Law Hill looks down over a familiarly harsh and rugged view into the Shibden Valley. Emily managed to hang on perhaps six months here, collecting no reserves of happiness but gathering and mulling over images and stories connected with the place, for future use. High Sunderland Hall, nearby, has features in common with the architecture and history of Wuthering Heights. Carved in seventeenth-century stone it bears a Latin motto whose translation is:

> This Place hates, loves, punishes, observes, honours
> wickedness, peace, crimes, laws, the virtuous,

which can be read in two ways: either downward, coupling 'hates' with 'wickedness' and so on, or across, in which case one has the impression that generations of the malign and the decent arbitrarily mingle in these walls which have a law of their own, disinterestedly tolerating good and evil, sanctioned by no civil or divine authority save the will of the inhabitants, and insulated like those of the Heights in Emily's novel. She will have heard too the story of the predatory orphan, Jack Sharp, aptly named, who milked the estate, persecuted the relatives and all but destroyed his benefactor's property, Walterclough Hall. Charlotte wrote to Ellen Nussey, hearing of Emily's 17-hour working day, 'This is slavery. I fear she will never stand it', and Emily made again for home, along with Branwell, whose career as a Bradford artist was no sort of success. Judging by the sour expression on the face of one of his sitters, Mrs Kirby, his landlord's wife, not to mention her memorable head-dress which resembles the plumage more

normally associated with an Indian chief, Branwell may have
made the mistake of treating portraiture as if the sitter had the
slightest interest in receiving a realistic image rather than a
flattering reflection. The artist now applied himself to the
consumption of opium, which, because it was considered to be
both an acceptable pain-killer and a universal panacea, you could
buy over the counter from the pharmacist, as laudanum or in
tablet form, for a modest sum. Life was now imperceptibly
darkening and closing upon Emily and her family. Visits from
Ellen Nussey and the emergence of a new curate in the light-
hearted and flirtatious person of William Weightman in 1839 gave
a superficial pleasure. Yet the need to find some fixed plan to
provide for their futures was constant and pressing. In 1841,
Emily recorded with vigorous optimism the plan to found a school
between them, securing an independent livelihood. Her
perception of the value of money and her dexterity at handling it,
which would later enable her to manage the investment of Aunt
Branwell's legacies with genuine interest, is suggested in her hope
that in four years' time 'Our debts will be paid off, and we shall
have cash in hand to a considerable amount.' She looks toward the
future with a determined optimism, as if defying it to contradict
her hopes, but ready enough to cope if the project misfires. Her
stoically fatalistic 'Time will show' contrasts poignantly with the
worry and dejection of Anne's paper, written that same evening in
Scarborough: 'What will the next four years bring forth? . . . How
will it be . . .?' Emily is writing from a position of security, in the
stronghold of Haworth, Anne worn out amongst strangers. With
her usual honour and loyalty to her 'twin', Anne acknowledges:
'all are doing something for our own livelihood except Emily, who,
however, is as busy as any of us, and in reality earns her food and
raiment as much as we do.' It was as if Anne had to cover up a
moment's resentment that Emily's frailties allowed her to remain
at home, lingering in a perpetuated childhood. Emily must have
felt the same, with a grief that propelled her to Brussels with
Charlotte to finish her education at the Pensionnat Héger.

Emily was now 24. Her new teacher (with whom Charlotte was
to fall fruitlessly in love) was an intellectually gifted person, whose
scintillating mind was lodged in a temperamental personality. He
bullied, pulled faces and was irate. This made Charlotte laugh,
but 'Emily and he don't draw well together at all', she wrote, with
what seems likely to have been a grand understatement.

Nevertheless, it was also true that 'Emily works like a horse'. M. Héger was approached by Mrs Gaskell years after Emily and Charlotte were both dead, and asked for his opinion of his pupils. His remarks, though possibly fossilized somewhat by time and moulded by awareness of the transformation of pupils into famous authors, is interesting. His idea of Emily was that she should have been a man. Emily would not have thought much of this. He had observed her defiant eccentricities, her philosophical and argumentative skills, and concluded that she was a unique species. He saw in her a rare logical power, an exploratory mind (as well as advocating an exchange of sexes, he thought her talents might have been usefully employed as 'a great navigator'), and an imaginative ability so genuinely original that it would be automatically and universally persuasive in changing a person's mind. These are potentially dangerous gifts, perhaps, for they all stress power. M. Héger qualified his praise of Emily somewhat drastically by calling into question her moral character, which was in his view 'egotistical', tyrannizing over the more feminine and yielding Charlotte. He was not quite wrong in any of his judgments. Emily's extraordinary logical grasp is evident to us in the intellectual perfection of the structure of *Wuthering Heights*. She was, in a buried sense, already 'a great navigator', not only of the inner Pacific where Gondal had been discovered but also in guessing a route to areas of the psyche that are not commonly registered or charted. The despotism which she exerted over Charlotte was of the sort of 'egotism' which might animate a drowning man who lunges at the nearest floating object and sticks to it in a frail hope of surviving. The 'great navigator' of M. Héger's rhapsody was (as Nelly says of Catherine bathed in tears at her time of extremity) 'no better than a wailing child'. Throughout her time in Brussels, Emily was engaged in a mortal struggle for breath and to keep her hold, so that she would not go down altogether.

A memoir by one of the pupils Emily taught reads as follows:

I simply disliked her from the first; her tallish, ungainly ill-dressed figure contrasting so strongly with Charlotte's small, neat, trim person, although their dresses were alike; always answering our jokes with 'I wish to be as God made me'. She taught my three youngest sisters music for 4 months, to my annoyance, as she would only take them in play hours so as

not to curtail her own school hours, naturally causing many
tears to small children . . .

This wholesome and broad-minded person displays several of
those attributes of female charm that must have goaded Emily
Brontë (and indeed any sensitive person) to the quick. Laetitia
Wheelwright embodies the ideal of the 'lady-like' to perfection.
First and most importantly, Emily looks so hideous. Then, she
cannot take a spiteful joke in good part, and is consequently to be
thought of as lacking in courtesy. Lastly, she is deliberately mean
to young children. This is the case against Emily Brontë, which
must have provoked in her an angry and hurt desire to 'cast the
world away' again for good. The opportunity to do so, and to leave
behind for the rest of her life the genteel standards of Brussels,
came with the death of Aunt Branwell in October, 1842. Emily
returned with Charlotte to enter into possession of a workbox with
a china top and an ivory fan, which were the keepsakes
bequeathed to her in Aunt's will, together with the more
substantial legacy of a share of £350 each in her aunt's small
capital, to be invested and to stand between the young women and
destitution if the worst came to the worst. It was a year of losses,
for William Weightman had died the previous month, inflicting
on Anne an unhealing wound, and depriving the whole family of
an atom of its frugal share of light-heartedness which it could not
spare. With Aunt Branwell dead, and the stiff backbone of the
structure of home suddenly weakened, it was easy to see that
Emily ought to take her place and move indoors, to manage the
domestic arrangements of the Parsonage. She was able to spend
the whole of 1843 fruitfully isolated in Haworth, Charlotte having
returned to Brussels, Anne and Branwell tutoring at Thorp
Green. For all the effect that Brussels had upon her, she might as
well never have crossed her own doorstep; and with her usual
methodical application she wiped her mind clear of traces of the
experience, as if it had been a stain or smear upon her memory.
Emily's roots were strictly local. Returning to Yorkshire this time
was like coming of age, for she was now in control of the
household, totally free to come and go between the house and the
moor. Her poetic gift was given scope to ripen so that now, in her
mid-twenties, she was writing a poetry of deepening maturity and
philosophic spirit. She came close to her father, acting as his eyes

for him as his blindness increased, and playing Mozart, Haydn and Beethoven on the piano in his study. After her death, he had the piano removed upstairs so that it should not recall to him with unbearable vividness the memory of Emily playing. It seems very true to her character that Emily should have excelled at the piano, since music is of all the arts most close to mathematics, and Emily Brontë of all literary artists most immaculately logical. The will to order, whether in the practicalities of house-work or the making of a poem or novel, was uniquely strong in her.

This will to order, sustained by her new liberty and independence, seems to have surfaced in the isolation of 1843. Having re-rooted herself and asserted her identity and security at home after nine months in a very foreign country, she felt free and confident enough to pause and assess her own work on a self-critical principle. In February, 1844, she collected together all the slips of paper on which her poetry had been written, sifted, selected and ordered it, and began to copy the poems which she thought worth keeping into the two flimsy note-books whose quality would be flattered if one called them 'humble'. These manuscript books are limp, small and faintly-lined, purely functional receptacles, one for '*Emily Jane Brontë*. GONDAL POEMS', the other for more personal lyrics. Emily had two distinct styles of handwriting, just as she had two worlds, one of 'reality' and the other of 'imagination'. Longhand was for the everyday world. A miniature print was for the world of her poetry, to suggest a 'published' effect as in the tiny books manufactured by the children in early childhood, and also probably to render the specialness of every word in this undertaking. Emily's handwriting in her notebooks is spidery and cryptic. Her title 'Gondal Poems' announces itself with endearing childishness within a surrounding of clumsy flourishes embellished with a little tracery of leaves. This homely elaboration in one who stood always for the plain and the austere even to the point of barrenness suggests how much the transcription of these poems meant. The poems are copied carefully and proudly, but they are not easy to read. Their privacy is paramount, and she did not seek to pass them around or design them for any eyes but her own. Yet these two notebooks represent a significant step from the personal toward the public world. Unlike the sealed Diary Papers in which Anne and Emily had wrapped the most sacred trivia and the highest hopes of their lives, Emily had now made the deliberate choice of perpetuating her personal fantasy-world into the future in a form that was open rather than closed, for it declared itself in a convention that any author or reader would recognize and could relate to. This is exactly what happened when Charlotte ('accidentally', she said) came upon the Gondal notebook in September or October, 1845, read all forty-three poems and wrenched Emily Brontë's poetry out into the light of day. Emily had laid herself open to such ambush, 'casting the world away' with one hand only.

Charlotte's prodigiously 'accidental' reading of these forty-three poems convinced her that these were 'not common effusions, nor at all like the poetry women generally write. I thought them condensed and terse, vigorous and genuine'. When she confronted her sister with her discovery, Emily reacted with a high rage lasting days at what she saw as a rape of her privacy and a betrayal of trust. Charlotte had reached through the window of Emily's safe-keeping of her secrets and ransacked what was there. Poetry as a hoarded personal secret is a precious but vulnerable gift. Emily must have feared that once it was raised to the surface from the mine which only she could visit, its colours and meanings would fade. She interpreted Charlotte's 'accident' as an act of aggression, sabotaging the balance she had elaborately achieved between inner and outer worlds, turning her inside out. Something of the fury with which she turned on her elder sister might also perhaps have stemmed from a sinister sense of excitement at having been discovered and praised, and feeling her worth recognized. Emily in a fit of anger must have been very daunting indeed, if her 'normal' behaviour is anything to go by. Nevertheless, Charlotte, bred of the same resistant stock, simply weathered the storm, keeping up a forceful debate with her sister, to the effect that she should publish. Then Anne quietly appeared with a selection of her own poems for Charlotte to consider. Emily felt able to pool her resources in the family of her sisters' poetry, finding there a necessary safety in anonymity: she agreed to join the corporate speculation, though probably with the grim reservation that she would have to count the exposed poems as spent and rely on her inward resources to mint new meaning.

Yet she had committed herself to the world outside, and it marked an epoch in all their lives, parallel to that moment in

which the poetic spirit in the form of twelve wooden soldiers had
borne in upon the emotionally destitute children when Emily had
been 7 years and 11 months old. Now, at 27, she was willing to
pour out something of that spirit, in a time of new harrowing.
Charlotte had been rejected by M. Héger; Branwell had collapsed
into alcoholism and drug addiction, dismissed by his employer
and covertly rejected by his employer's wife. He descended upon
the family home in 1845 and in his mental agony and drug-
derangement set about wrecking its peace, night and day. His
sisters oscillated between compassion at his ruin and disgust at
the obscene pointlessness of the destruction he underwent and
caused. Patrick Brontë later took him into his own bedroom at
night, to try to contain his son's suicidal and other manic
tendencies, and endured with him the night-horrors of drug-
dependency, from which the young man would emerge each
morning mumbling the somewhat inadequate tribute, 'He does
his best, the old man'. The 'old man' who was required to do his
best was 70 years of age, a period not commonly well adapted to
the physical wrestling bouts and total sleep-deprivation of nursing
an addict. We need to realize that Branwell's shattered
personality noisily dominated each room of the sanctuary for the
next 3 years to understand the conditions under which his sisters
composed their great novels, quietly contradicting through the
structural perfections of a reflective art the squalor of their
immediate surroundings. Volubly cursing and kicking his way
round Wuthering Heights, Heathcliff doubtless re-enacts some of
the madhouse antics with which Branwell had enlivened her
home, until such behaviour might have come to seem normal and
expected. This turbulence, and a sense of communal failure and
shame, is the background against which we may read Charlotte's
account of the deep bond of authorship into which the three sisters
now entered:

> We had very early cherished the dream of one day
> becoming authors. This dream, never relinquished even
> when distance divided and absorbing tasks occupied us, now
> suddenly acquired strength and consistency: it took the
> character of a resolve. . . . Averse to personal publicity, we
> veiled our own names under those of Currer, Ellis, and Acton
> Bell; the ambiguous choice being dictated by a sort of

conscientious scruple at assuming Christian names positively masculine, while we did not like to declare ourselves women, because . . . we had a vague impression that authoresses are liable to be looked on with prejudice.

Emily's first part in the realization of this dream was the inclusion of 21 of her poems (lightly revised) in a volume *Poems by Currer, Ellis and Acton Bell,* published by Aylott and Jones at the authors' own expense in late May, 1846. Here was a way for Emily to enter public life without being judged by the extraordinary criteria of the state of her hair or the amplitude of her dress. Just as her father in inviting her to declare her views from the cover of a mask twenty years ago had thoughtfully provided the means of freedom of speech with impunity, so the masculine-sounding 'Ellis Bell' masked Emily Brontë, emancipating her from the demands of the lady-like and the scrutiny of the impertinent. Neutrality of gender, with suggestions of androgyny, was also perfectly fitting to Emily's concept of the eliding of male and female into the ungendered soul. 'Ellis Bell' was rather a genuine embodiment than a covering pseudonym for 'Emily Brontë'. Reviews of the poems were favourable, especially of Emily's contribution; sales so poor as to be ludicrous, perhaps even hearteningly funny to the new poets themselves. They sold two copies. The cash investment sank without trace. But the spiritual investment was richly yielding. Under the impulse of this first initiative, each began to write a novel, Emily's *Wuthering Heights* being composed probably between the autumn of 1845 and her twenty-eighth birthday in 1846. A year later, the publisher T. C. Newby accepted the dog-eared and unsavoury-looking manuscript of *Wuthering Heights* and *Agnes Grey* which had been sent on the rounds of various publishing houses and rejected, while declining Charlotte's *The Professor.* Charlotte's second work, *Jane Eyre,* was printed the same year with another firm.

From this point, 'the Bells' became public property. Emily's and Anne's publisher let them bear a proportion of the costs which he neglected to refund. He cashed in on the resounding success of *Jane Eyre* by spreading the insinuation that there were not three Bells but one Bell, and that Bell was the lucrative Currer. Emily, despite (or more probably because of) pressure from Charlotte to move from this shoddy dealer to her own fair-dealing house of

Smith, Elder, stuck with leech-like obstinacy to her own charlatan, rather than take on someone else's patron. For her it was axiomatic that first ties are best, and that you do not break them even in the light of experience. Independence from the well-meaning and sensible interferences of Charlotte in her business was beginning to take on the status of a life's work. Probably, she never felt that her note-books were safe again. Emily's novel was considered by the critics to be a rather nasty freak. They drew attention to the disgusting, inhuman, evil, uncivilized and artistically immature qualities of *Wuthering Heights*, but promised readers a treat if they were looking for something completely new, 'for we can promise them that they have never read anything like it before'. An American reviewer deduced from his perusal of this grotesque novel that the author, though an unusually gifted man, was 'dogged, brutal, and morose'. This villainous individual read the reviews of 'his' work with deep pain and disappointment. Charlotte told Mrs Gaskell years later that all the pleasure of the excellent reception given *Jane Eyre* was drained for her 'in seeing Emily's resolute endurance, yet knowing what she felt'. Emily had not known herself to be 'dogged, brutal, and morose' before these reviews told her so. Whereas she had understood that she could not appear as anything but a misfit in relation to what was expected of orthodox females of her age and class, it now came as an extra blow to find that she could not keep intellectual and emotional company with the male of her species either. Perhaps she did not belong to, or in, this species at all. Yet she offered Newby another novel, and seems to have begun composition, so that there is no suggestion that she felt dispirited enough to withdraw from the powerful challenges and excitements of authorship. Any such withdrawal would have been out of character. Instead, she withdrew spiritually into a deeper sealing of her personality, especially against Charlotte who was so helpful, and so solicitous, and so patronizing. When Charlotte, in London with Anne, in the self-regarding heat of the moment rashly blurted out the secret of Emily's identity to their own publishers, and then revealed to Emily that this violation of her privacy had occurred, she provoked another fit of ire which seems to have left her feeling shaky and alarmed in a quite new way. She wrote to Mr Williams:

Permit me to caution you not to speak of sisters when you write to me. I mean, do not use the word in the plural. Ellis Bell will not endure to be alluded to under any other appellation than the nom de plume. I committed a grand error in betraying his identity to you and Mr. Smith. It was inadvertent—the words 'we are three sisters' escaped me before I was aware. I regretted the avowal the moment I had made it; I regret it bitterly now, for I find it is against every feeling and intention of Ellis Bell.

Not only was Charlotte betraying Emily's secrets without permission and therefore putting at risk the inner security through which Emily managed to keep herself stable—breaking Emily's code without warning, at random—but she also held rather a critical view of Emily as a novelist, and conveyed this eroding view (based on the supposedly untempered 'harshness' of her work) to her sister. There is a peculiar desolation in Charlotte's account of Emily's flaws of character in her memoir of 1850, as if she were still arguing with her inflexible sister over the edge of the grave, and imploring her to recognize that Charlotte had only wanted to do her good. She said that her sister had been a 'hero' but had no fund of 'worldly wisdom', and that 'An interpreter ought always to have stood between her and the world.' This was what Charlotte had tried to be, and got no thanks for. It was the last thing Emily had ever wanted.

But publishing affairs were suddenly cast into the background of the Brontës' lives, as they approached in 1848 the crossroads of their existence as a family. Branwell's head-and-shoulders sketch of his bespectacled person, with curly and apparently thinning wisps of hair upon his forehead the only reminder of the Bonaparte image of childhood, preludes a letter of January, 1848, to one of his drinking friends. It is captioned, '*Patrick* Reid "turned off"', without his cap. 1848', and features him with a noose around his neck, ready to be hanged. Beneath, orgying young men lurch backwards off their chairs, grouped around a pub-table on which a punch-bowl spills. The inebriates are labelled Sugdeniensis, Draco the Fire Drake, St John in the wilderness, Phidias and 'St Patrick alias Lord Peter'. Vestiges of Branwell's swash-buckling Angrian games hold company with his dear love of ancient art (Phidias was the architect and sculptor of Ancient Greece), and a prevailing sense of a Christian retribution whose victim Branwell is, by virtue of his sufferings in the cause of sin. He has gone to the bad, an anti-Christian martyr. During this year, his world contracted to the practical problems of laying hands on 'Five pence worth of Gin in a proper measure'; his body became emaciated; his mind foundered in delirium tremens. A new wave of losses was now commencing, which would be final for Branwell, Emily and Anne. Branwell, contrite and softened in heart, died on Saturday, 24th September. 'Nothing remains of him but a memory of errors and sufferings', wrote Charlotte, who sought to console herself for the loss of her childhood twin with the thought that Branwell was better off dead, considering his abuse of his status as 'his father's and his sisters' pride and hope in boyhood'. Emily's reactions have not been preserved, but it seems impossible that the author of *Wuthering Heights* and the poems could have shared such a view. She reduced no fellow being to the sum of his failures.

At Branwell's funeral, Emily is supposed to have caught a cold. By late October she was suffering from pain in her chest, shortness of breath and a hacking cough. She was thin and white, and obviously entering the terminal stages of a tubercular illness at a hectic pace, whilst refusing to discuss her illness or to see a doctor. Emily raised her difficult and intractable nature to the status of heroism in the silent fortitude of her dying. But heroism is invariably hard on those who, loving the sufferer and longing to share the pain, are repudiated by an impersonal assertion of dignity. Emily made no concession to her disease, getting up unaided every morning at 7, feeding her animals and sitting up until 10 at night until the day of her death. On the morning of 19th December, it was obvious that Emily could not outlive the day, the death-rattle being already heard in her throat as she rose and dragged herself downstairs. Charlotte went out onto the moors, combing around for a last, late-flowering spray of heather to bring the moorland world indoors for her dying sister. Against the odds, she found such a flower but Emily was beyond caring. She died on the sofa in the front room at two in the afternoon. Anne was to follow her into death 5 months later; Keeper, who howled outside Emily's door every night for weeks after her loss, outlived her by 2 years. Tabby died in 1855; and Charlotte the same year, in childbirth. Only Patrick Brontë, the sole long-lived member of his

family, survived hale and tough in the Parsonage in company with
the absences of Maria and her six children, until he was 85 years
old.

   Charlotte's letters telling her friends and acquaintances of
Emily's death immediately after the event, and the memoir she
wrote to accompany the 1850 edition of *Wuthering Heights* and
Agnes Grey, rise to the level of a requiem. The letters are set out in a
prose as plain, terse and austere as the character of the woman
whose death they announce, and speak with a grandeur as fine as
anything Charlotte ever wrote. The personal loss expresses itself
not in rhetorical outbursts or elaborations of feeling but with the
regularity of a heightened pulse-beat. The short sentences break
simple, ordered statements of fact upon their reader. Each is like
an act of will, charged with the stress of withheld emotion. In her
refusal to yield to grief, Charlotte, who uniquely understood her
sister, released and celebrated Emily's own energy:

> My Dear Ellen,—Emily suffers no more from pain or
> weakness now. She will never suffer more in this world. She is
> gone, after a short, hard conflict . . . Yes; there is no more
> Emily in time or on earth now. Yesterday we put her poor,
> wasted, mortal frame quietly under the church pavement.
> We are very calm at present. Why should we be otherwise?
> The anguish of seeing her suffer is over; the spectacle of the
> pains of death is gone by; the funeral is past. We feel she is at
> peace. No need now to tremble for the hard frost and the keen
> wind. Emily does not feel them.

Later in the cycle of her grief she would feel a sense of unity in the
vanishing of her four sisters and her one brother, as if they were all
part of a constant process of unreality:

> It is over. Branwell—Emily—Anne are gone like dreams—
> gone as Maria and Elizabeth went twenty years ago. One by
> one I have watched them fall asleep on my arm—and closed
> their glazed eyes— I have seen them buried one by one—

Charlotte in her solitude perceives herself as if in the posture of a
mother whose function has been to recurrently close the eyes of a
succession of young beings eliminated over a twenty-year period
for no reason that she can conceive: she links the new deaths,
including Emily's, to the oldest losses of all, those of the children

Maria and Elizabeth, deeply buried in her consciousness but never outlived. These two eternal children, stabilized forever at the ages of 10 and 11, are now joined by a new generation of young adults. For Charlotte in her extremity, condemned to live, the image of her beloved family as having only the status of 'dreams' is a negation of their reality. But for Emily, to have entered the condition of dream, as her poetry and *Wuthering Heights* assert, is to be reborn into a new and more fully real state of being than anything we can imagine here. Dreams, leading the soul out of the exile and singleness of incarnation, pass through the walls of flesh and connect the homing spirit with the deepest sources and affinities of its nature. Her redemptive vision includes the assurance of a final meeting with kin; a shaking loose into a new freedom, on open moorland.

PART TWO

HER POETRY

4 *Earth Rising To Heaven*

Riches I hold in light esteem
And Love I laugh to scorn
And lust of Fame was but a dream
That vanished with the morn—

And if I pray, the only prayer
That moves my heart for me
Is—'Leave the heart that now I bear
And give me liberty'.

LIBERTY was not only a state of mind to be entered into, but
inhered in a local place to be visited. Emily Brontë's boast of being
untouchable by the preoccupations with wealth, love and fame
which animate the inferior majority of people was fortified by the
accident of place which provided an area literally on Emily's
doorstep, in which she could breathe oxygen that had been
through no one else's lungs, for hardly anyone ever went there,
and move freely and haphazardly because there were no rights of
way. This place of liberty, upon which she founded her conception
of beauty and her idea of value, and which became essential to her
continued health, was the moorland behind her home. The poem
above, written at the age of nearly 23, admits that she had been
aware of impulses to be economically independent; to seek love; to
be known. In place of these transient whims has come an
undivided and serious aim, to be left alone. She wishes to be an
outsider, because going outside was, literally, pure joy.

Haworth Parsonage and Church stand on the border of the
village whose cobbled main street fell steeply down to the valley,
flanked by terraced weavers' and wool-combers' cottages of
massive local stone, and crowded with 4,000 inhabitants living in
great squalor. Outside the front windows, an army of Haworth
dead reposed under dark wedges of stone without a blade of grass
to be seen. This crazy-paving of gravestones prevented the
decomposition of dead bodies from going ahead at a healthy pace,
and the arrested putrefaction was fed into the well which some
aberrant engineer had sunk into the graveyard and out of which

61

the village drank its water. Typhus was endemic. In the vault of
the church itself other corpses lay, exuding the scent of
putrefaction into the nostrils of the worshippers. Haworth could
claim to be one of the most unhygienic corners of England, full of
overflowing cesspits and middens which made it prudent to tread
carefully along the road. Infant mortality stood at 41%. Emily as
a little girl looked down from the parlour or nursery window upon
this prospect. But on the other side of the walls bounding the
graveyard, like a great sea of grass and heather, Haworth Moor
washed cleanly up against her world. It rose gently beyond the
house, dipping and then inclining into the wilder, exposed
countryside of Penistone Hill. From here she could walk directly
onto adjoining moors, founded on the same sandy, acidic soil
formed by the kind of rough stone which is called millstone grit.
There is not much that human beings can do with infertile and
barren moorland except quarry for rock, and this was done in
Emily's day: the cold flagstones paving the floor of her home, as
well as the pavements of the village, the gravestones and the
squared stone of which the houses are built, were all hewn out of
the moor. Or one could dig peat to burn; or simply walk out across
the moor seeking solitude.

Oddly, except perhaps in *Wuthering Heights* which is like an
extended nature-poem in novel form, Emily Brontë was not
primarily a nature-poet. Her lyric gift expressed itself either in
personal statements or in dramatization of Gondal conflicts: it is
rarely descriptive. Her poetic forms and rhythms are simple and
bare, founded on ballad, very tense and stressful. Often, her voice
is heard to falter or stammer; the poems may suddenly terminate
in mid-thought as unsatisfying fragments; metrical effects may
appear gauche or clumsy. Yet in her apparent defects as a poet is
rooted the grandeur of her most powerful utterances; hesitant
rhythms assume the immediacy of irregular breathing. Rather
than providing full-scale descriptions in sensuous terms of the
moors she so loved, her poetry is concerned with a philosophy of
nature, telling of the relationship between inner and outer worlds.
She sometimes shows you the details of the scenery but more often
the long vistas of heathland whose large spaces correspond with
areas of deep quiet within the introspective self. This loss of
identity in an absorbing landscape was something she had felt
from her earliest days. She was 20 when she wrote:

I'm happiest when most away
I can bear my soul from its home of clay
On a windy night when the moon is bright
And the eye can wander through worlds of light—

When I am not and none beside—
Nor earth nor sea nor cloudless sky—
But only spirit wandering wide
Through infinite immensity.

Not to be, or to be bodiless, is here to be 'happiest'. An idea of
what she might mean by the abstraction 'infinite immensity' is
given by the denial of earth, sea and sky as wholes in favour of
spaces bounded by no limit, compared to which earth, sea and sky
would appear too detailed and specific. To reach this
contemplative ideal in which she could be released into the form of
a wandering spirit, Emily had wandered for many miles around
the countryside surrounding Haworth, forgetful of self, and
conscious only of immense horizons. Clues to the freedom she
seeks here had been sensed in the solitude of the high moors.

It was not only the large planes and surfaces of the moors which
she loved, but also their colour and detail, and the few animals
whose habitat is there. The purple heather, calluna, which covers
the moors and the bilberry bushes which offer a kind of manna in
that wilderness of heath, are often mentioned in *Wuthering Heights*.
These are the principle source of colour. When the bilberries are
ripening, they turn from green to red to black: after fruiting
prodigally in July and August they turn bright lime-green leaves
to a violent crimson, then fall back into the encompassing
darkness of the moor in winter. Their taste is sharp and rinsing.
The moor is fundamentally a benign place, both for Charlotte and
Emily Brontë. In *Jane Eyre*, Charlotte's heroine finds in her
destitution that she can bury herself in heather for warmth, and
take handfuls of berries to sustain her. The moor is a final place of
safety against exposure, a resting-place. For Emily too, the moors
mean rest, clement on the very verge of annihilation. At the end of
Wuthering Heights the graves of Linton, Catherine and Heathcliff
are to be crept over in course of time by the grass and heather of
the moor. There are no hideous flagstones committing their
inmates to the eternally cold mercies of their architecture, but
rather the organic absorption of those persons into the peaty moor

itself, secure and wholesome. The grass which covers the graves, simple and common as it is, is a manifestation of the natural world which Emily contemplated with love and respect. On the moors below Haworth and toward Hebden Bridge, where the earth is undrained there are silver acres of cotton-grass, known as 'bog-baby-warning' according to an old and sensible coinage, for the bogs with their strange clumps and tumuli of grasses and reeds are dangerously full of concealed streams. But in the drier ground above Haworth, which Emily associated with safety, freedom and beauty, there is a wealth of grasses—tall tussocks which dry in autumn and winter into beautiful pale golden or whitish masses, and areas of delicate couch-grass whose seeded heads shine in wind and sun; and the strong common grass which in one of the most exquisite imagist fragments in our language Emily makes it possible for us to see in a new light:

> Only some spires of bright green grass
> Transparently in sunlight quivering.

This is the whole of the poem as she has left it to us. It justifies its brevity through the initial 'Only'; this is all we shall be seeing. It may stand for us as a kind of key-poem in assessing her attitudes to language and nature. We remember the laconic Emily who was often thrifty with her language to the point of rudeness. Not only is the subject deliberately commonplace but drastically limited in scope: not a vista of grassland but only 'some' blades of conventionally 'bright green' grass—a small number of ordinary things offered in wilfully tautologous terms. However, these are not 'blades' of grass: they are 'spires'. Emily's proudly sacramental view of nature is declared: each grass-blade is shaped like the spire of a church (Catherine would be happy to see the church brought crashing down on her grave in *Wuthering Heights*). The low plant we tread upon, which can get its root down into any crack, is raised by Emily to the status of something holy. It 'aspires' like everything in the world of her imagination. Heaven is brought down to earth and rooted in its sour clays: she will not look into the musty old air of church buildings or the even poorer, darker air of religious dogmas to perceive Heaven. Her heroine Catherine is very clear that 'Heaven did not seem to be my home', for after dreaming that the angels flung her down to earth since she could not accommodate herself to the Afterlife, she wept with

joy to find herself on the coherent earth. In what was possibly the
last poem she composed, she wrote that:

> The earth that wakes *one* human heart to feeling
> Can centre both the worlds of Heaven and Hell.

For Emily the earth, as it is, has Paradisal qualities, so that the
Christian idea of Heaven becomes an unnecessary fiction and that
of Hell a moral irrelevance. She is one of the great iconoclasts of
our literature.

But these 'spires' of bright green grass with which Emily
replaces the sterilities of orthodox Christianity are only raised
high because the observer is willing to be brought low. If you try to
imagine yourself seeing that transparent greenness of the few
grasses, you realize that they must be observed close-up, and that
you must lie down on the ground to achieve the fullest view. Only
this posture makes it possible to look into and through the leaves,
charged with the sunlight that discloses their form and colour.
The most telling word she retains for the last: it is 'quivering'. The
beauty of what Emily sees on the moors around her home, and
which in the deepest sense is her home, derives from the fact that
nothing in that world is ever static. She centres her faith not on the
mausoleum of the church, enshrining perishable old ideas, but in
what moves and is alive now, and in this moment. She hates the
letter and loves the spirit; is almost physically sickened by forms
and formalities, both socially and in religious matters, driving
always toward the vital, organic life of ideas. In Emily's blade of
grass the 'quivering' motion tells of a vital principle which she can
feel on her own skin, intuit from the trembling responsiveness of
nature's most modest productions. It clothes itself in the massive
shapes of the hill-sides shouldering up against the sky, their backs
turned on human, civic or social concerns. Equally, it clothes itself
in the vesture of a tuft of grass, transiently illumined, and of no
account in itself. It is found in the fast and icy winds which flow
over the moors at all seasons, flattening the aspiring grasses and
driving the rare hawthorn trees 'all . . . one way' like the gaunt
trees at the Heights. It is found in the impulses, passions and
fantasies which appear in the mind of the observer of all this
excited life, and overflow into a verse which contains and 'curbs'
the will of the imaginings. The gentle tremor in the grass-leaf
belongs to this process of response, self-assertion and the testing

out of forms of being against a situation that is elementally open.

The openness of the countryside around Haworth affects any observer. The moors are open to both sky and wind, the sky being most commonly a moving one, characteristically grey or overcast, with clouds passing away across the horizons. Rock, heather and whin are hammered to such a degree by prevailing winds that it is natural that only tough, fibrous and hardy species survive easily; rocks are weathered out; the country undulates into small troughs and clefts where there is peace from the wind. It is very silent, except for the calling of the birds whose homes are built within the heather: the curlew or the lapwing or peewit, which vault into the air emitting piercing, rhythmic calls. These birds are important symbolic presences in *Wuthering Heights*. It is said that Emily came to know, through walking around the moors from her tiniest childhood, every clump of heather, outcrop of rock, cleft, gulley and stream. Ellen Nussey, Charlotte's friend, who came as a rare visitor to the Parsonage, recorded the joy which Emily seemed to feel when she walked out onto the moors, shedding her brooding indoor self, to talk and laugh more freely. Ellen's account, given late in life, after all the Brontës were dead, in attributing to Emily a suspect 'gleesome delight', not to mention a 'lithesome, graceful figure' and charming smiles, seems touched with a nostalgic sentimentality consonant with the conventionality of the raconteur. Nevertheless, Ellen has obviously not invented the account of Emily at 15 when she first visited, actually volunteering to take this stranger out for a walk, and opening up into a uniquely communicative mood, impressing the visitor with the geniality and vigour of her mind. Charlotte's nervous enquiry when they got back as to 'How did Emily behave?' has an authentic ring. Ellen also spoke of their walks to a number of secret and precious spots where memories had been accruing from deepest childhood, such as Sladen Beck and a stream with a waterfall which the children called 'The Meeting of the Waters':

> It was a small oasis of emerald green turf, broken here and there by small clear springs: a few large stones serving as resting-places; seated here, we were hidden from all the world, nothing appearing in view but miles and miles of heather, a glorious blue sky, and brightening sun. A fresh breeze wafted on us its exhilarating influence; we laughed

and made mirth of each other, and settled we would call ourselves the quartette. Emily, half reclining on a slab of stone, played like a young child with the tadpoles in the water, making them swim about, and then fell to moralizing on the strong and the weak, the brave and the cowardly, as she chased them with her hand.

We glimpse here, coming out of hiding, the poet who celebrated 'All Nature's million mysteries—/The fearful and the fair'. 'The fair' is of course easy to love, and is an obvious feature in this refuge of bright green turf surrounding the meeting streams. Emily's joy in the beauty and clemency of the natural world appears as the setting of many of her Gondal poems, in the 'spell in purple heather' which acts to bind the observer in a trance, or in the harebell on its 'slight and stately stem':

> The buds hid like a sapphire gem
> In sheaths of emerald hue.

She speaks of these as 'breathing upon' the human heart, to awaken and warm it into life. In a later Gondal poem she lists the benign relationships between the animal- and the moorland worlds:

> The linnet in the rocky dells,
> The moor-lark in the air,
> The bee among the heather-bells

These small processes of interaction within nature are felt as too perfect in themselves to need embellishment. Nature is sensed as a pattern of gentle intercommunications between different kinds of individuality.

Ellen's recollection, however, also seems to touch on that other, far less palatable mystery of nature, of which Emily's poetry did not simply take account but also made its preoccupation, the mystery of 'the fearful' aspect of nature, the predatory reality which may underlie any peaceful scene, or that mingling of awe and disturbance with peace in a scrupulous person's awareness of landscape. Emily is remembered lying out on a stone, dangling her hand in the water like a god from another element, and teasing the underwater creatures, meanwhile discoursing upon 'the strong and the weak', disturbing the creatures' habitat so as to test out their relative powers of adaptation and survival. Ellen says she played 'like a young child', but she is also seen studying animal behaviour with an analytic, scientific eye and hand, devising parallels with the behaviour of human animals swimming around in their element. It is very like the deadpan detachment with which she recounted scenes of obscene violence and cruelty in *Wuthering Heights* : Hareton hanging puppies, Heathcliff 'grinding down' his victims. Emily was aware of a power and violence within herself which matched that element of 'the fearful' within the natural world, and her lack of inhibition and fear relating to it was raised to the status of a philosophical principle. In one of her French essays written in Brussels, she wrote that 'life only exists upon a principle of destruction', so that it is clear that both personal intuitions and observations of natural processes had convinced her very rational mind of a view closely resembling that which would be elucidated as a scientific theory 15 years later by Darwin in *The Origin of Species* as the law of the survival of the fittest. The weak lose all. The strong inherit the earth. It would have been thought an unforgivably unwomanly point of view, as well as an offensive unchristian heresy.

The problem for Emily Brontë lay in deciding who were to be thought of as 'the fittest'. I think she schooled herself in a compassion that would be based on this natural principle of 'the strong and the weak' but which would stretch to embrace both—predator and prey, aggressor and victim—in equal measure. In a Gondal poem of 1839, 'Well, some may hate', aged 21, Emily's persona deliberately revises an instinct to sneer above the grave of a weak and vain person, on the following grounds:

> Do I despise the timid deer
> Because his limbs are fleet with fear?
> Or would I mock the wolf's death-howl
> Because his form is gaunt and foul?
> Or hear with joy the leveret's cry
> Because it cannot bravely die?
>
> No! Then above his memory
> Let pity's heart as tender be:
> Say, "Earth lie lightly on that breast,
> And, kind Heaven, grant that spirit rest!"

The deer's timidity is inherited and constitutional, but so is the wolf's carnivorous appetite. To the final howling of the wolf is added the unbearably high-pitched shriek of the baby-hare, caught in a trap or animal jaws. Compassion is universally and equally apportioned—to the killer and the prey, since both are helpless, at the mercy of inborn responses and inherited conditions. Emily Brontë's vision of the state of nature here is that of one who sees the subjection of all species to the law of universal carnage, where only the strongest survive, but where the strong are not lovable (the wolf) and their survival is only temporary. Strong and weak in the animal world are subject to the same law, and cannot choose an attitude or stance. Human nature is genetically determined too, so that the dead man, like the young hare, had been born lacking the power to resist his fate or stifle his frailties. Few people have ever had such an absolute conviction of being among the strong as Emily Brontë. But this was only moral strength because it learned to acknowledge the claims of the weak. Her poem, like so many others, is in the form of a debate, in which the persona presses the case for compassion and tolerance against something deeply inhumane which lies within himself. I think it represents Emily's own conflict in coercing herself to abandon or mitigate an instinctive ungentleness toward common frailty, a search for sympathy with those who are voluble in their sufferings, or who cannot make grandiose or epic claims for themselves. Her physical and mental stoicism was so extraordinary that it seems she had constantly to reattune her mind to the evident fact that such qualities must always be rare. In this poem, she records a grudging but successful attempt to concede to the common average. Emily would make several high claims for her superior calibre: 'Riches I hold in light esteem', 'No coward soul is mine', and these are perhaps her most famous utterances. But her moral greatness as a poet is rooted in her desire to temper her own pride, recognizing kinship with her race rather than claiming exemption. In strenuous contentions between opposing principles within herself, she uses her will to gainsay her will. She is a dualist who systematically forces herself to respect opposites, generating energy from them: in *Wuthering Heights*, both the raw, wild power such as Heathcliff embodies and the 'Linton' qualities of temperance, kindliness and traditional good feeling are acknowledged and polarized. She does not choose the one and abandon the other, but with artistic patience and discipline sustains our sense of the worth of each in its own terms. At 18, she had concluded a poem:

> True to myself, and true to all,
> May I be healthful still,
> And turn away from passion's call,
> And curb my own wild will.

She had then perceived that being true to one's own nature, the deepest obligation in her private code of values, depended on being 'true to all'. Her moral strength lies in her 'curbing' and containing of her energies, mocking her own taste for the daemonic and the superhuman, relating her fantasies to the down-to-earth, putting down her own rebellions. The world of nature from which she learned so much about 'the strong and the weak' also taught her the necessity of a universal and inclusive compassion.

Yet this violence had its own natural opposite within her, coexisting with a wistful, tender lyrical gift, an eye for the vulnerable and delicate, both in nature and in human relationships. Ellen had spoken of seeing Emily and her younger sister constantly 'twined' and 'twinned' in one anothers' arms as they walked out onto the moors. Emily appears in an attitude of loving kindness with one who was her apparent opposite, inseparably together with this tenderly loved different personality. If Emily loved the moors in their large, dark and wilder manifestations, she also cared for them in detail, for the bright and miniature flowers which belong to the exposed heathland just as familiarly as the coarser scrub, grasses and heathers. In *Wuthering Heights,* one of the most touching moments is Edgar's bringing to Catherine in her illness 'a handful of golden crocuses' in March, which she identifies as belonging most powerfully to the moors: ' "These are the first flowers at the Heights" '. In his final sentence Lockwood notices the harebells amongst the heath and grasses; the second Cathy has teased Hareton by endowing his porridge with a crop of primroses. These small flowers have the status only of fragile moments, evanescent in the expanse of heath and rock which spreads like an eternity full across the vision of *Wuthering Heights*; but they are included, instinct with their own particular meaning. In the poetry there is a recurrent awareness of the beauty of this kind of detail—tiny bells of ling, a heavy raindrop burdening a spray—details which gain in intensity by being able to assert themselves as individuals in the midst of an undefined wilderness. They contribute to a sense which Emily Brontë as a poet everywhere conveys, that nature is finally consolatory and welcoming to man, even in his mortal moments. Images of extreme cold, inimical to life, carry an extraordinary visual beauty and accuracy:

> Then let us sit and watch the while
> The blue ice curdling on the stream.

The tough and fibrous stem and branches of the winter heather, stripped of blossom, are seen as the cradle for a love-child:

> Forests of heather, dark and long,
> Wave their brown, branching arms above.

The debate beginning 'In the earth, the earth', in which two voices argue over whether it is preferable to live or to die, conceives of the mingling of human remains with the underworld mesh of grass-roots as an image of harmony and union:

> In the earth, the earth, thou shalt be laid,
> A grey stone standing over thee;
> Black mould beneath thee spread
> And black mould to cover thee.
>
> "Well, there is rest there,
> So fast come thy prophecy;
> The time when my sunny hair
> Shall with grass roots twinèd be."

The sombre absence of colour in the first stanza, 'grey . . . Black . . . black', is implicitly contradicted in the second which manages to yield an impression that the hair which twines with the unseen living roots of grass (as the hair of two people used to be woven together and secured in a locket) will retain its 'sunny' character, like buried gold. The grave, in which the corpse is pictured as sandwiched between two layers of ugly 'black mould' by the admonitory voice, becomes connected with another kind of living process. Nature is felt, both above and below ground, as man's original and final home, in which he comes to terms with the mystery of the 'fearful'.

Emily seems to be reaching constantly toward a statement about the natural world which will be satisfying because it is inclusive, bearing the stress of opposites. An image by which she conveyed this union was that of the wind. On the moors above Haworth, at a high altitude above sea level, it is not possible to avoid for long the wind that hammers against the open ridges of heath. Such violent winds are a contributory cause of the formation of heather-moors on the gritstone and limestone high ground of Yorkshire. With recurrent fires, they have prevented the growth of trees in these areas and opened the way on that shallow, peaty, acid soil for heath to develop, so that above the arable meadowland of the valleys (characterized as the 'Thrushcross' element in *Wuthering Heights*), the countryside has become as it is as a direct result of its lack of protection from high winds which make it hostile to other forms of vegetation. Literally, the wind is the breath of life to the moorlands to which Emily devoted herself. Of the four elements, earth, air, fire and water, it is air which predominates in her work. The wind may be felt as killing, or as bracing; you may perish with cold from it, or be inspired with exhilaration. Emily Brontë recognized both qualities in a willing paradox. For her, the wind was symbolic of the creative imagination, powerfully and invisibly driving its transforming force through the objects of contemplation. She admired and felt that some principle within her echoed the racing of the wind across the surface of the earth. It was like the careering of Eternity into time which was the pivot of her visionary experiences. The root of the word 'wind' in Hebrew has the same meaning as our word 'spirit', and this fruitful pun which is traditional in Christian tradition, is a coincidence on which Emily Brontë drew. 'The wind bloweth where it listeth' is rendered in some Biblical translations as 'The spirit bloweth where it listeth'. The wind is liberty; and to stand in it is to be free. It is also the unifier and reconciler in Emily's vision, like Wordsworth's idea of a spirit which 'rolls through all things' in *Tintern Abbey*. But because Emily Brontë was always thinking not of an abstract 'spirit' but of a wind localized in Yorkshire, a real blustering force which you have to resist in order to maintain your own stance, her conception of this old idea has a powerful originality.

The high winds around Penistone Hill and Withens (the supposed original for Wuthering Heights) are relaxing because the necessity for keeping upright entails forgetting to be conscious. They disperse consciousness; cleanse and renew. These are the feelings and experiences Emily is drawing on when she has Catherine, dying from the suffocation her nature feels in the enclosure of Thrushcross Grange, battle to get the window open, so that she can take some of this vital air into her lungs:

> "I'm sure I should be myself were I once among the heather on those hills . . . Open the window again wide, fasten it open! Quick, why don't you move?"
> "Because I won't give you your death of cold," I answered.
> "You won't give me a chance of life, you mean," she said, sullenly.

Ellen is right to say that the freezing blast will kill Catherine, physically; Catherine right to insist that to drink that air will heal her, spiritually. The tragedy lies in the fact that the two modes of life are shown as not consonant. To achieve the life of one, you must lose the other. To 'be oneself' is the most invincible problem raised by the novel. To 'be herself' Catherine knows that she must go back; go home. Emily's novel reveals the fatality involved in growing up, being consigned to time. Nothing can be unwoven, for the web of destiny has been spun, measured out and will be cut. Catherine yearns, ' "I wish I were a girl again, half savage and hardy, and free" ', for this is the only way one could get back. She feels that the wind, coming in from her home on the moors, is somehow the clue to getting back across the abyss. It is, but only through the process Ellen so sensibly counsels against, by killing her. In Emily Brontë's novel, the grief is that though we contain and in essence still are the child in whose form we set out, this is a solely interior condition, revealed in dreams which 'kill . . . with desire'. Though it may be theoretically possible to recreate childhood, babyhood and even embryonic experiences, this can only be subconsciously or through the quickened memory, for there is no permit available from adult life back to the Eden of childhood. Adult life is shown by Emily Brontë as a condition of forfeit and exile—exile even from 'being oneself'. Catherine cannot rejoin Heathcliff in the old way of life: she is married, pregnant, ill and mortal. Heathcliff cannot undo his separation from Catherine in her life-time, for the same reason, and after her life-time because that requires that he survive 'with (his) soul in the grave', and, obviously, ' "I *cannot* live without my life! I *cannot* live without my soul!" ' But there is a suggestion that there does exist a path home on two levels: through that chill, inhuman wind turning one's life to air, returning one's body to the mould; through giving birth to a new identity. Catherine is displaced to the younger Cathy. A new child goes out into the world; makes for the Heights instinctively, where the wind's source is. When Cathy grows up in her turn, she expresses her dream of Paradise as involving:

> rocking in a rustling green tree, with a west wind blowing, and bright, white clouds flitting rapidly above; and not only larks, but throstles, and blackbirds, and linnets, and cuckoos pouring out music on every side, and the moors seen at a distance, broken into cool dusky dells; but close by, great swells of long grass undulating in waves to the breeze . . .

The west wind associated with the return of spring, and with the extravagant symphony of birdsong (song itself is air), co-exists in this poetic speech with one of the most accurately observed and naturalistic images anywhere in Emily's works, the sea of grass blown upon by the wind. For Cathy as for the author, Paradise is a condition of resolute wakefulness; nothing is quiescent or acquiescent. The wind has turned the acres of meadowgrass to a billowing sea, 'swells . . . undulating', as the invisible force which animates all existence miraculously reveals its presence through its effect upon the visible, pressing down and releasing the grasslands in a rhythmic succession of waves of energy. A violent force expresses itself in effects which are soft to the eye—absolute power; absolute gentleness. This commonplace sight on the hill-sides around Haworth is looked at with a fresh, transforming vision.

Ten years before she wrote *Wuthering Heights*, at the age of 18, Emily wrote for the first time on this subject of the spirit-wind, in a precocious bravura-piece. Her poem releases tidal waves of images, in which the wind turns the land to a sea; the normal oppositions and incoherencies between things are beaten down. Contrarities fuse and flow together:

High waving heather, 'neath stormy clouds bending,
Midnight and moonlight and bright shining stars;
Darkness and glory rejoicingly blending,
Earth rising to heaven and heaven descending,
Man's spirit away from its drear dongeon sending,
Bursting the fetters and breaking the bars.

All down the mountain sides, wild forests lending
One mighty voice to the life-giving wind;
Rivers their banks in the jubilee rending,
Fast through the valleys a reckless course wending,
Wider and deeper their waters extending,
Leaving a desolate desert behind.

Shining and lowering and swelling and dying,
Changing for ever from midnight to noon;
Roaring like thunder, like soft music sighing,
Shadows on shadows advancing and flying,
Lightning-bright flashes the deep gloom defying,
Coming as swiftly and fading as soon.

Emily celebrates liberty as change. The energy of the wind
abolishes distinctions in the natural world, so that earth meets
heaven, water overpowers earth, time accelerates, the shadows of
clouds pour over the earth as if in a speeded-up film. Her poem's
rhythms stream over the hypnotically repeated feminine rhyme in
a virtuoso outpouring. Each time the present participle sounds, it
enacts the moment of release, the ecstatic breaking loose of spirit
from body like the tumultuous upheaval of a storm. For Emily,
even at this comparatively early age as a poet, the active spiritual
principle is seen as imprisoned in the static physical one. The
source of the joy which moves the poem is that the wind can 'burst
the fetters and break the bars' of the heavy clay into which human
consciousness is perpetually sinking. There is an assurance that
some principle within the natural world is there to breathe upon
and recreate the torpid human clay, making undulations in the
visible world (like those which Cathy sees in her mind's eye as
waves in fields of long grass) whose rise and fall 'Shining and
lowering and swelling and dying', makes darkness tolerable and
'dying'—of sound, of life—welcome, if it is a movement toward
something else. The wind whips each creation into an impulsive

statement of its own nature, so that it can be itself. Flattening the
heather it also lets it go, to stand up for itself in a sea of motion and
tumult as 'High waving heather'. She captures too those days of
mingled sun and wind in which clouds chased by high winds cast
rapidly moving areas of cold shadow which may be seen
approaching from a distance across what comes to seem more a
lightscape than a landscape. In this life-long excitement, Emily
Brontë saw earth rising to heaven and heaven descending to earth,
as if one only needed to go out of doors to be directly free.

5   *These Straining Eyes*

While gazing on the stars that glow
Above me in that stormless sea,
I long to hope that all the woe
Creation knows, is held in thee!

And this shall be my dream to-night—
I'll think the heaven of glorious spheres
Is rolling on its course of light
In endless bliss through endless years;

I'll think there's not one world above,
Far as these straining eyes can see,
Where Wisdom ever laughed at Love,
Or Virtue crouched to Infamy

The satisfactions and excitements of the natural world, with the
hints they carried of an entire liberation, were contradicted by an
equal longing for peace and oblivion. The conscientious, wakeful
spirit reveals a constant desire for sleep, together with a
dissatisfaction with the world as it is which cannot be answered by
an astringent blast of air upon the moor. Many desolating
thoughts about the worthlessness of the race to which she
belonged and the need to dream herself out of the condition in
which she is implicated, moved Emily Brontë to take refuge in the
search for another world. An instinct that such an alternative
world was tantalizingly real and accessible caused her to strain
her eyes to glimpse what might lie beyond the veil of the senses
which blurs the soul's perceptions. As a fantasist, she had
invented Gondal, but Gondal was a recognizable world with a
network of roots in the disappointments and imperfections which
characterize the 'real' world: lost love, lost virtue, infidelity,
bereavement. As a visionary poet, calling on the fantasy world she
had woven, she sought to evolve an eyesight adapted to an ideal
reality, and a light beyond our common darkness. In *Wuthering
Heights*, Catherine, coming near to the border of this ideal through
her terminal illness, senses its proximity 'through the walls of an
aching heart', but this contact with the visionary world leaves her

77

raw since she is walled in by the flesh which only touches upon reality to be exacerbated by it. In dying, she feels she will be 'really with it, and in it'. The visionary spirit in Emily's poetry is in this way allied with a death-wish. Rest and peace are associated with insight. Nearly as profoundly as she is a poet of the moors, Emily Brontë is a poet of the night.

Traditionally, night is the feminine time; day the masculine. The moon's silver light is a transforming medium in which we are released from daylight distinctions. Babies are most commonly born at night, magic is worked, and dreams conceived. The ancient female deities, Diana the virgin huntress, goddess of liberty, the woodlands and animals, protector of all human femininity; Ceres the goddess of fruitfulness; Lucina to whom mothers call in childbirth; Proserpina the female power of the underworld, are all lunar. Emily Brontë's most sacred imaginings occurred by night in waking meditations on the edge of trance, lying on her narrow camp-bed by the window in the silence under the stars. In the poem I quoted above, fugitive before her futile consciousness of the sufferings to which all sentient living things are prey, she turns away from the 'dark' world of daylight to enter a state of musing reflection:

> How clear she shines! How quietly
> I lie beneath her silver light
> While Heaven and Earth are whispering me,
> "To-morrow wake, but dream to-night".

'She', the moon, is the feminine principle associated with the soothing process of what Emily here calls 'Fancy', elsewhere 'Imagination'. By 'dream' she does not necessarily mean the dreams of sleep but rather that kind of thought which is a gentle process of reflection or brooding meditation, associated from most ancient times with creativity. The moon has immemorially been related to the sea as agent of birth, drawing its tides, an image which Emily characteristically transforms so that the moon herself appears to swim in a 'stormless sea' of night sky. The poet whose affinity was with storm now reveals herself as having an equal and balancing affinity with the tranquillity of a condition of stormlessness. Tumultuous seas of heather and grassland yield in the nocturnal poetry to a calm ocean whose most comforting attribute is the stasis of circular movement, the orbiting planets which never deviate and are detached from all earthly conflicts. It is clear that compassion for the universal sufferings of the creatures of earth hurt Emily Brontë. A practical nature like hers would feel especially offended at the thought that there was nothing to be done about it. Her fiercely pre-Darwinian perception that life exists on a principle of bloodshed gave no genuine pleasure to an essentially kind nature. In her reverie she tries to imagine that beyond this planet there exists no such thing as suffering: in other galaxies the planets revolve exempt and intact from the contamination of the pain that covers the surface of our earth. The tentativeness of this belief is admitted in the conditional expression, 'I long to hope'. The power to hope is withheld.

In another poem, written in 1845, three years before her death, she mourns the return of morning-light, when night-thoughts must go into abeyance. She inclined to personify her visionary experiences, and here the stars are eyes, steadfastly watching over her in a vigil which gave her such safety that she could afford to take spiritual flight:

> Ah! why, because the dazzling sun
> Restored my earth to joy
> Have you departed, every one,
> And left a desert sky?
>
> All through the night, your glorious eyes
> Were gazing down in mine,
> And with a full heart's thankful sighs
> I blessed that watch divine!

The stars do not look 'at' but 'in' to her. She turned abruptly to avoid the probing eyes of strangers, but imagines that there are eyes in the universe which look upon her lovingly and can be responded to. Her 'God of Visions' in 'O thy bright eyes must answer now' solicits on her behalf. In 'To Imagination', this watching and benevolent presence is 'my true friend', speaking with 'kind voice'. The eyes of the hypnotic stars which persuade her of a friendly presence in the universe beyond our gravitational field are another manifestation of this inward resource, whose source is the deepest and least understood area of the psyche, but which also mirrors some state of peacefulness accessible outside.

In 'To Imagination', that classic, rational and balanced defence of imagination as an alternative faculty to reason, she insists on the untrustworthiness of the imagination, for it frames a world which we urgently want, but in which we cannot physically live and be sane. Whereas Branwell had been seen falling headlong into the trap of trusting the fantasy-world without reservation, Emily recognizes that this world of 'hovering visions' belongs exclusively to evening; is subjective and delusory if it is not controlled and structured by a will which is firmly grounded in commonsense. Commonsense is not a tedious virtue for Emily Brontë, but indispensable for survival and never to be lightly discarded:

> I trust not to thy phantom bliss,
> Yet still in evening's quiet hour
> With never-failing thankfulness
> I welcome thee, benignant power,
> Sure solacer of human cares
> And brighter hope when hope despairs.

Only at night, when the world's business officially closes down, is it safe for the soul to come out of hiding to contemplate the open eyes of the stars. When the human race has shut its eyes corporately, the poet can allow herself to be off-guard, and there is licence to 'be oneself'.

The quality of the peace sought by Emily Brontë in the watches of the night is specialized and idiosyncratic, exactly as you would expect. For it seems—in a way that is impossible to paraphrase—to involve its own opposite. Her idea of peace as a dream-world which underlies our waking consciousness like a great and unexplored sea is evoked but not explained in her night-poem 'Ah! why, because the dazzling sun'. Under the influence of the guardian stars:

> I was at peace, and drank your beams
> As they were life to me
> And revelled in my changeful dreams
> Like petrel on the sea.
>
> Thought followed thought—star followed star
> Through boundless regions on,
> While one sweet influence, near and far,
> Thrilled through and proved us one.

The sense of freedom she expresses is paradoxically attained in terms of the two most turbulent and least homely elements, air and water. Dreaming is like being out at sea: there is no map, nor an expectation of being able to navigate, since there are no rational landmarks. Passive in the unpredictable dream-world, the dreamer does not know what will happen next. No coherent or chronological narrative is either possible or wanted in dreams, and all you are able to say about them is that they are 'changeful'. The poet is free to enjoy the excitement because, being perfectly adapted to survive in these elements, she has nothing to resist there and no anxieties. The dreams are at once experienced as a visitation from an exterior power and as being unmistakably one's own. Storm and flood are the major images here: the elements which traditionally threaten the light boat of human existence. Emily asserts herself not against but within these 'hostile' elements by declaring herself a native of them, designed not only to prosper but also to 'revel' there. The image of her voyage through the strange ocean of dreams as a 'petrel on the sea' is an almost miraculously appropriate emblem of the adaptation of a living individual to the violent currents which are its home. The storm-petrel of which she is thinking has great and enduring powers of flight, and rides gales inches above the sea, its feet just skimming the surface below the deep keel of its body. Sailors, observing the bird's apparently supernatural powers of riding out storms without danger, had named it after St Peter, who, imitating Christ, was able to walk out upon the surface of Lake Gennesareth without sustaining harm. Emily Brontë, in taking that ancient sacramental bird as a means of showing her joy in flight, explores the active and positive aspect of her yearning for night. It is peace conceived not as a lethargic sinking to rest but as a rising to act out her being. She conveys also her isolation; the petrel is the unaccompanied bird whose path, because it has to be guessed against the adverse and random forces of tempest, must be peculiar to itself. M. Héger would say that Emily should have been a great navigator or discoverer. In fact she navigated only the private seas within, guided by the constellations of the night-world in which 'star followed star/Through boundless regions on'. As the petrel treading the surface, Emily also expresses her sense of invisibility, her contempt for surface appearance in the emblem of this modest, dark bird. Under cover of its own sombre exterior it acts out a uniquely virtuoso personality.

But the poem is less about Emily Brontë's search for anonymity and effacement than about the frustration of that need by an antagonistic force which is malign to the soul's deepest hungers, and can push through the walls of the self to invade the private world. She writes of a rape, of night by day; stars by sun; female by male. As the sun comes swelling up, it seems engaged on assault, and breaks the course of gentle and regular meditation. The creative 'feminine' world is violated by the masculine:

> Blood-red he rose, and arrow-straight
> His fierce beams struck my brow:
> The soul of Nature sprang elate,
> But mine sank sad and low!

The imagery consciously arouses suggestions of rape. The sun is male, for 'he' rises; is 'blood-red', suggesting mutilation; it aims like an arrow, purposefully and with a 'fierce' striking action inspired by enmity. The poet of nature acknowledges herself to be at cross-purposes with a Nature which welcomes the invigorating warmth. She evades its light, searching to regress into the night-time, but the sunlight invades even her closed eye-lids and forges through them. The rape-image is exactly right for this sense of vulnerability, experienced as physical sensation, as of the exposure of delicate tissue to rough intrusion:

> My lids closed down—yet through their veil
> I saw him blazing still;
> And bathe in gold the misty dale,
> And flash upon the hill.

She closes her eyes against the glare of unwanted sunlight, but the lid of the eye is thin and translucent, built to exclude only a limited intensity of light. Through the tiny capillaries of the eyelid, the sun filters in to a show of dusky red colour from which the retina has no means of escape. Inevitably, Emily recognizes, her vision is going to be dispersed by supervening facts (facts which commonsense knows really ought to be welcomed), and there is no guarantee that with the coming of a new night the capacity to dream and 'see' in that inexplicable way can be restored. The sun is a symbol of that force of active consensus which can make her see in the way 'he' and not she chooses, blinding her to the inward visions, scorching with a penetrating light and sexual heat the 'cool radiance' of the distant self in timeless contemplation:

> O Night and Stars return!
> And hide me from the hostile light
> That does not warm but burn.

This poem most forcefully demonstrates Emily Brontë's impulse to defend her vision; the insecurity of the dreamer or visionary who has to live in the so-called 'real' world which can make no allowance for the dissenting kind of perception to which she is committed. Ironically, it also reveals, through recounting the undignified details of her attempts to escape the dawn by burrowing down into the bedclothes, a recognition that her preference implies an element of inversion or immaturity. Most people, she is aware, would know what to think about those who are so fond of their hallucinations that they would seek an eternal night in which to 'revel' in them, and commonsense would be with them.

Emily's attitude to 'most people' is not as simple as it seems at first. Valuing commonsense as she did, it could not be one of dismissal. She never claims to be unique in her capacity for visionary insight, despite her arrogant statements to the effect that other people's religious beliefs are crack-pot by comparison with the 'God within my breast'. Her pretensions, it is true, are—if you reduce them to paraphrase—gross. She calls 'my own nature' an adequate guide to behaviour for the reason known to children of all ages that 'It vexes me to choose another guide'. The opinion is stated in 'How beautiful the earth is still' that the majority of us are:

> Poor slaves, subdued by passions strong,
> A weak and helpless prey

when contemplated alongside her own abstinence in keeping out of the run of normal human activities on the infantile principle that, if you don't commit yourself to wanting something, you can't be disappointed. But there are two voices in this poem, each anonymous. One questions; one replies. The two disclose long and impersonal vistas in the private world. Rather than sealing her vision away like an embryo curled defensively upon itself, the poet willingly opens it out. Images expand in this inner space until

they are uncontainable any longer and break into immense
abstractions. The persona says that she:

> "with firm foot and tranquil face
> Held backward from the tempting race,
> Gazed o'er the sands the waves efface
> To the enduring seas—
>
> "There cast my anchor of Desire
> Deep in unknown Eternity;
> Nor ever let my Spirit tire
> With looking for *What is to be.*
>
> "It is Hope's spell that glorifies
> Like youth to my maturer eyes
> All Nature's million mysteries—
> The fearful and the fair—
>
> "Hope soothes me in the griefs I know
> She lulls my pain for others' woe
> And makes me strong to undergo
> What I am born to bear."

The first voice had spoken of the many as 'Poor slaves',
superciliously; the second expresses sorrow amounting to real
pain at sympathy for the griefs of the many. The first voice is
harsh; the second, though remote, is kind. It is the second voice
that carries the vision, so that, looking through her eyes we could
almost 'see' Eternity, as a place, with dimensions ('Deep'), whilst
remaining aware that what we are looking into is 'unknown' at the
very moment of our perception. The seas of Eternity, washing out
the lettering of time, have a strange dimension, as if perceived
through a looking-glass; she casts anchor in an element that is
without stability or measurement, expressing a serene but hard-
won trust that the creatures of time can reach by act of will out of
this dimension, to secure themselves in Eternity. In 'Death, that
struck', the branches of time are seen as taking their vital sap from
'the fresh root of Eternity'; the dead tree will go back down to
nourish its source. Emily Brontë opens up her inner life and allows
it to be read, trustfully, and with a feeling of safety, though it is full
of secret places and fearful landscapes, oblivion, alienation. The
grave is there too, but it is organically linked to an Eternity in

which she can, as if existentially, find final safety where there is neither form nor face. She looks toward the seas within, willing to commit herself to the anonymity of the deep rather than join in the games on firm land which so soon run themselves to a standstill. It is interesting that she speaks of the sea of eternity as 'effacing' the sands of time. That fear of effacement, losing face, is one of the archetypal fears to which human beings testify. Emily had felt in social life this threat of being seen 'effaced', literally, as having no face, as Virginia Woolf felt, and is represented as feeling, in her sister Vanessa's portrait of her with her features blanked out. Yet Emily Brontë is unafraid of the elemental agent of effacement, the power of death, interpreting this power as the synthesis of all contending energies.

The ethic of personal stoicism, combined with the refusal to sympathize with one's fellow mortals to the point at which this becomes personal pain of the indulgent and useless sort, are appropriate to a mind whose happiness derives from detachment from the business of life. The claim to be 'different' and even arrogantly superior to the majority is generally just a sturdy and candid statement of a perspective. Despite the frequently withering remarks at the expense of the many, Emily Brontë is in a very real sense speaking with a universal voice. The plainness and impersonality of her style, unvarying from character to character or between points of view, is oddly void of personality. Additionally, she is conscious of containing more personalities than a single self, being either a corporate 'two-in-one' or even a sacrilegious 'three-in-one'. In 'The Philosopher's Conclusion', structured again as a debate between voices, she says that:

> Three Gods within this little frame
> Are warring night and day.

> Heaven could not hold them all, and yet
> They all are held in me
> And must be mine till I forget
> My present entity.

This was written in 1845, within a year of *Wuthering Heights*. Her nature is a battle-ground between three distinct identities, imagined as having superhuman power and status, as 'Gods', and threatening the frail structure in which they are incarnate. Her body is a 'little frame', alluding perhaps to the small structure of a woman's body, inhabited by the powerful resources of a woman's spirit. In the absence of the creative principle which could unify this three-fold nature in a sea of reconciliation, the 'space-sweeping soul' who is the major persona of the poem seeks the oblivion of death, the forgetfulness and anonymity of an appeased but unsolved struggle. The 'conclusion' to which the philosopher has arrived is the death wish. It is better to conclude life altogether if existence must be lived on one's nerve-ends, in a state of continuous and irascible self-division. The 'conclusion' is inserted within the second voice as an italicized refrain:

> *"O for the time when I shall sleep*
> *Without identity,*
> *And never care how rain may steep*
> *Or snow may cover me!*
>
> *"No promised Heaven, these wild Desires*
> *Could all or half fulfil;*
> *No threatened Hell, with quenchless fires,*
> *Subdue this quenchless will!"*

Again, the poem is a dialogue between opposite points of view uttered by like voices, suggesting an identification beneath superficial variations: 'soul' or 'spirit' rather than individuality, and a dialect that can be used to express those 'eternal rocks beneath', the archetypal in human experience. The 'conclusion' is boxed within the frame of reported speech. The framing of narrative within narrative in *Wuthering Heights,* in which stories and voices enclose and include one another like a nest of Chinese boxes—so that one can hardly tell which interpretation or event is intended to be 'inside' and which 'outside'—reinforces a similar sense of anonymity. So does the preference for the ancient folk-ballad forms speaking for a common rather than a singular experience; a race rather than an individual; 'us' in 'me'. It is a form which has traditionally been linked with dream, vision and the supernatural. 'I' who dream, see visions, and am taken up in supernatural events am a core 'I', the root of self in the subconscious mind and in communal history rather than the civilized, particular 'I' who happen to enter the waking world at a specific moment. Emily Brontë chooses this impersonal 'I' through whom to live out her visions on paper, so that the reader feels the openness of the personal pronoun, its readiness to include her or him.

This disqualification of no one from the power to dream is beautifully exemplified in *Wuthering Heights* when Lockwood, blundering into a world of which he understands little or nothing, thinks that the genteel tea-party manners and expectations of urban middle-class society might be a way of introducing himself to Heathcliff's home and family. The uncouth details of the Heights are seen by him through the refining lens of the couth society from which he has come. There is a pile of dead rabbits in a corner, but Lockwood sees it as a cushion on which repose a cluster of charming cats assumed to be Cathy's pets. Cathy he identifies first as Heathcliff's 'amiable lady'; then as Hareton's 'beneficent fairy'. She is rude and sour but he insists on identifying her as a respectable married woman, meek, obedient and acceptable. Anyone can see that the Heights is a rough place, anyone including Lockwood: he does not acknowledge it at first because he does not want to. Its reality defies both his expectations and the social order which serves him as a survival plan. Mincing, grinning, lisping outlandishly in his (to them) barbaric southern English dialect, Lockwood seems to stand for all which lies outside the visionary world of Emily Brontë's poetry and fiction—and, standing outside, cannot participate. Yet it is the fact that Lockwood does, physically, come into Wuthering Heights; awkwardly introduces himself; enters the bed-chamber in which the elder Catherine lived and wrote; gets in to the oak press which is within this bed-room; gets in to her diary, scribbled down the margins of a sermon-book; enters physically into intimate contact with the inner visionary world of Heathcliff and Catherine which is so strange to his nature. He also enters emotionally (falling for the younger Cathy in his own limited way), and—most crucially—spiritually. Lockwood, in Catherine's bed, enters into the dream that belongs to her and Heathcliff. Her ghost calls to him personally: he hears, sees, touches her in his dream. He is scared so badly that he involuntarily performs one of the most cruel actions in the novel— getting hold of the child's wrist, he rasps it 'to and fro till the blood ran down and soaked the bed-clothes'. It is vigorous, purposeful, continuous. Heathcliff never does anything so shocking.

Lockwood, daintily taking tea and mouthing only the most neutral conversation, could never have been imagined as performing an act of violence, or dreaming an interesting dream. Yet what he does is made to seem an intrinsic part of his nature: it is true to his character. It would be true to ours, if we were there and could be observed in that underlying world of the subconscious mind, playing out our fears and desires, across the threshold of conscious inhibition or taboo. By including Lockwood who as narrator mediates between their inner and our outer reality, Emily Brontë makes a statement about human nature in general. It is a fabric universally capable of visionary experience. If Lockwood, then all of us. She opens a door through which each reader may enter into parts of himself kept previously dark and unknown because we have not wished to be introduced to them. Both the novel and the poems are about 'going in'.

If we ask for literal description of this visionary world, and wonder what exactly it was that Emily Brontë saw there which was worth the forfeit of the commoner forms of success and pleasure, there is likely to be frustration. Her mature art was bound up with an attempt to describe the process of 'seeing' in this way, suggesting structures or metaphors through which it could be imagined, and formulating attitudes to it: saying what it felt like before and after it was over; what difference it made to life; how to live with such visions. But speaking so continuously about her visionary life, she never told what she could see. Emily was in the dark when it came to expressing such visions; she conceived of herself as being imprisoned. Words are part of the fetters which bind the soul to the corporeal world, since they have not been forged in order to communicate and frame a mystical experience. The personal poems identify the onset of such visions with night-time, semi-darkness and moonlight. The Gondal poems repeatedly offer a situation of a young girl incarcerated in a dungeon: Emily's heroines thus enthralled speak defiantly; Anne's tend to lament. Darkness within an enclosure makes possible intense privacy, cessation of action and of participation in the affairs of the world, accompanied by a drowsing openness to musing thoughts. She lodges what is perhaps her most suggestive description of the structure of visionary experience in an otherwise highly unremarkable Gondal poem of 1845, 'Julian M. and A. G. Rochelle', written in a crudely regular ballad jingle and involving the melodramatic visit of Lord Julian to the Gondal heroine's place of living interment. After several stanzas of that metricated groaning called for by the plot, the poem opens out unexpectedly into an exquisite lyricism. The persona asserts the existence of a 'messenger of Hope', mediating between the captive and a freedom more absolute than anything conceivable by those at liberty in the outside world:

"He comes with western winds, with evening's wandering airs,
With that clear dusk of heaven that brings the thickest stars;
Winds take a pensive tone, and stars a tender fire,
And visions rise and change which kill me with desire—"

'He comes': we are made aware of the visionary experience as being linked with a sexual approach, as if this were the closest 'normal' experience which the poet could think of to the meeting of self with other. The time of day is important, for it is transitional. Evening mediates between day and night: it is a middle state, of change-over, in which we may pass over a threshold or boundary. It mediates, just as the messenger does, between 'inside' and 'outside'. The west wind is traditionally associated with another mediating phase in the cycle of the seasons: spring-time which links the two extremes of the year. The atmosphere is of peace, a settling-down, for this wind is not tempestuous but gentle and seductive. It lulls even while it quickens the listening spirit. Emily Brontë suggests an openness and receptiveness which are not exposure to rough intrusion but a progressive state of clarification and enlightenment. The wind is connected with the source of light in stars; constellations seen thickly massed, remote but also 'tender': again, there is the suggestion of qualities associated with a human lover. The universe is perceived as protective, related to the solitary individual in a love-bond. The psyche, like the western winds that are 'pensive', is soothed into thoughtfulness. So far, the state is one of grateful relaxation—an awakening that is calm, moving upwards toward air and fire, away from the crass earth in which we are grounded. Yet in the fourth line an element more disturbing and exciting is introduced, associated with that 'change' which was celebrated in the storm-petrel image as bringing violent joy in the dream-state. This change brings arousal to a 'desire' which 'kills'. This may be understood by

comparison with sexual arousal, linked back to the tenderness
that provokes an initial want, and forward to the need that is felt, if
unsatisfied, as destructive physical pain. What is desired is—of
course—not said. What is seen is, equally, not described. This is
the first frustration of the experience: for the persona, in the killing
sensation of ungratified desire; for the reader, in the aroused and
unsatisfied urge to share what is being seen.

Emily Brontë now goes on to describe a second, and a
deepened, phase. The pain recedes, with any sense of an outer
landscape:

> "But first a hush of peace, a soundless calm descends;
> The struggle of distress and fierce impatience ends;
> Mute music soothes my breast—unuttered harmony
> That I could never dream till earth was lost to me.

> "Then dawns the Invisible, the Unseen its truth reveals;
> My outward sense is gone, my inward essence feels—
> Its wings are almost free, its home, its harbour found;
> Measuring the gulf it stoops and dares the final bound."

Again there is an act of mediation: the clearing of a passage
between opposed states of mind. In the first of these stanzas there
is a progressive closing down of the self against external noises:
'hush ... soundless ... mute ... unuttered', in order that
consciousness may be lost in a sealing-off of the psyche in trance.
There is a sense of relief in the dissolution of conflict. This is the
passage of initiation, before, in the second of these stanzas, we
move to the very centre of the vision. Here we might at least hope
to learn something of what the mystic 'saw', but that is not so. At
the crucial moment, she yields to the conventional negative
definitions to which mystical poets throughout history have—to
their own disappointment—resorted. What is revealed is 'the
Invisible, the Unseen'. When Dante reaches Heaven in his
Paradise he cannot look the huge light of the Deity in the face; in
Milton's Heaven, the angels surrounding their Maker cannot
suffer that intolerable light but cover their eyes with their wings.
At the height of the visionary experience there is something past
speech, beyond human eyesight and imagery, which may only be
described in terms of what it is not. We are none the wiser. If the
poet were to enter fully into the visionary world, she would never

re-enter our world at all, for the vision resides in a pool of absence, areas of stillness where there are neither objects, limits, self nor other. What Emily Brontë feels in this moment of vision is the most extraordinary sense of safety, as if she were going 'home', into 'harbour'. Her spirit is seen as a bird making ready for flight to its own habitat. The winged soul shakes free, preparing to fly into eternity. Remembering how deeply-rooted Emily's affections were in her own home, so that she cherished every detail of the moors amongst which she was bred, and literally wasted away if she had to leave, we may appreciate the extreme emotiveness for her of the words 'home' and 'harbour'. But she must encounter the bitter paradox of visionary experience in the recognition that she cannot yet go home after all. Like the ghost of the elder Catherine wailing outside Lockwood's window ' "Let me in" ', Emily's Gondal heroine finds herself a waif between the two worlds of the living and the dead. To merge with 'the Invisible' we must ourselves become invisible; must die. So far in the poem there have been paths or bridges between states of being, but there can be no final path save that of death. She must retrace her steps, go back the way she has come:

> "Oh, dreadful is the check—intense the agony
> When the ear begins to hear and the eye begins to see;
> When the pulse begins to throb, the brain to think again,
> The soul to feel the flesh and the flesh to feel the chain!"

Jolting, doggerel rhythms enact the indignity of collapse into consciousness, after the gradual unfolding toward revelation. The senses are raw and jarring in their impact on the open, oblivious spirit which has so deeply concentrated on its voyage of inwardness as to forget habits of self-defence. The Gondal prisoner comes hurriedly down to earth retaining no vestige of her dream.

Only in her novel, *Wuthering Heights,* itself a sort of dramatic poem, does Emily Brontë succeed in bringing to the light of day, intricately structured and coded with that secret logic of which the art of dream is master, one complete vision. The miracle is that she does so without draining the vision of its mythic power, as we so often do when in the cold morning light we 'tell' a dream to a listener and in the telling drain it of colour, reduce its power to bathos and blur its meanings until it seems a poor and

PART THREE

HER NOVEL:
WUTHERING HEIGHTS

6   *Baby-Work*

The Myth of Rebirth in Wuthering Heights

CATHERINE LINTON, as her mind turns toward its last agony, the departure from the 'little frame' in which the warring gods of her spirit contend, moves from violence to a disconcerting lull in which she starts to pull feathers out of her pillow and arrange them methodically on the sheet according to their different species. Her calm absorption in this work of sorting is more frightening than the hysterical fits that preceded it. It is almost as if she had broken through into another world or dimension, abstracted from the chronology of ordinary time, the limits of accepted space, into a quiet place which is inaccessible to anyone else, a sealed solitude. Nelly Dean, who watches and listens, is clearly alarmed and dismayed: she covers her sense of threat by labelling Catherine's occupation 'childish', a 'childish diversion'. She feels that if only Catherine—who is a nuisance— could be got to pull herself together and behave like a normal person, everything could be solved. Nelly's response is the sort that is appropriate and efficient in dealing with a small child's tantrum: you turn your back, avert your eyes and apply an abrasive scepticism. She is right in one sense that Catherine is being 'childish', for she has diverted herself entirely. She has gone straight through that invisible wall that separates our adult selves from our childhood selves, as if entering the looking-glass. In the looking-glass world (and Catherine is about to see herself reflected in the mirror which she takes for the old wooden press where she slept in her childhood) perception of time is altered. Childhood is now, immediate. But old age is simultaneous too: Catherine sees Nelly all grey and bent, as she will be, 50 years from this date. Catherine can speak back into the 'real' world from the dream-world, but she communicates as if from far away. All Nelly is definitely aware of is the chaos Catherine is creating in the room as she starts tearing feathers out of the pillow by the handful and scattering them wholesale, blithely unconcerned that Nelly is going to have to pick up the mess and put things to rights. (Nelly as narrator of *Wuthering Heights* is constantly concerned with tidying and putting to rights for Lockwood's and the reader's sake

95

the chaotic material of her story.) She feels cross and surly.
' "Give over with that baby-work!" I interrupted.' Getting hold of
the annoying pillow, she drags it by force out of the plucking
hands that are destroying it. All that she—and we—have to
compare such an irruption with is the destructive wantonness of
childhood in its 'baby-work', which is wanton because it does not
conceive of consequences. 'Baby-work' is an experiment on the
wrong side of the boundary between anarchy and survival. Yet the
minute we have heard Nelly reduce Catherine's strange activities
to this level, we know that she is wrong. We sympathize with Nelly
in her task of coping with the feather-spreading, uncontrollable
girl on the bed in her delirium: by making us wryly amused at her
predicament in the earthy Yorkshire idiom of her reaction to it,
Nelly also helps us to cope with it. But we have seen Catherine
expressing herself in an activity which cannot accurately be
construed as meaninglessly destructive. Beneath the elemental
tantrum is taking place a kind of 'work' which is mysterious and
purposeful. This 'baby-work' involves an urge toward a
fundamental and radical order, which underlies the common
'civilized' order and deeply criticizes it. Beside the work of sorting
and grading the feathers in the pillow, social order appears as a
kind of primitive chaos.

There is a very ancient story with its roots in Egyptian and
Greek mystery religions, of Psyche and a sort of 'baby-work' in
which she was engaged. Psyche, having lost her lover, Cupid, by
exposing him to light, was forced out of her cave into the terrible
light of the upper world. The vindictive goddess Venus gave
Psyche an impossible task to perform. She was given a huge heap
of mixed seeds to sort; a time-limit; and a threat of death in the
event of failure. Nobody could do what was required of Psyche: it
is not in human nature to fulfil this pointless and immensely
detailed task. Psyche was aided by the powers of nature. The end
of her story was initiation into full possession of her husband.
Psyche is the human spirit—our souls in their first rising to
consciousness, losing hold of our primal source and our first
intuitive affinities; forcibly separated from our twinned 'other self'
(Cupid); released into a light which we cannot love, for it exposes
us, abandoned and rejected, to a riddling life burdened with tasks
whose meaning is lost on us. Life is imagined as a quest, a seeking,
shot through with yearning. Yet some potent forces work for us,

mysteriously buried in the dark underworld of our nature, where darkness is creative; seeds are growing. The pointless 'baby-work' leads, as in all great structuring myths, to rediscovery, reunion and return in a changed form to an earliest truth with which we are finally able to deal.

The legend of Psyche is an allegory of the soul's expulsion, quest and reunion with the beloved. *Wuthering Heights,* with its story of Catherine's wilful separation from her 'twin', Heathcliff, her exile at Thrushcross Grange, the riddle of her delirium and the 'baby-work' of her pregnancy and delivery of the new Catherine, is an original myth of loss, exile, rebirth and return. It has the self-contained and opaque quality of all myth. It imagines the human soul as being female, seeking a lost male counterpart. The 'secret' of *Wuthering Heights* is not a displaced incest motif, nor is it a-sexual, as critics claim. Catherine, having betrayed the union with her own truest likeness, is involved in a sexual search, but sexual union is not the subject of the story, rather it is the metaphor for a search which is metaphysical and 'human' in the largest sense. Both Psyche's and Catherine's stories concern a metamorphosis. As the pupa opens to reveal the caterpillar, the caterpillar is bound into the chrysalis, and the chrysalis at its right season is unbound to reveal the new and sticky-winged butterfly which was there at every stage—an eternal and traditional image of rebirth—so Psyche must emerge; her world must darken and bind her; she must toil, despair, change, open, in order to rediscover. But she finds the beloved in her own person. Emily Brontë too stresses the suffering of those metamorphoses, the cramping pain of constriction, the terrible aspects of those rites of passage which initiate one into a new state. Catherine's is not a personal success-story like Psyche's. Emily charts two stages of metamorphosis: dead Catherine gives rite of passage to living Cathy. Like Psyche's the path is full of the most impossible riddles. She cannot trust her eyesight. The agony of death is the same as the agony of birth. It is dreadful to be born; hard to grow up; incomprehensible to die—and Emily Brontë will not say where exactly the new self in her myth of rebirth is located—whether in Heathcliff, in the second Cathy, in the heath where Catherine is buried. Emily preserves the mystery.

All along the way we are presented with images of the most astonishing beauty which, rooted in pain, loss and dissolution, bear suggestions of new life, and the release of the soul from the mortal carcass in which it is borne, as if waiting to hatch and fly. This is most deeply connected with the 'baby-work' of which Nelly complains so bitterly. Catherine reacts with ire to the thought of Edgar self-enclosed and adult, composedly reading in his book-lined study, for it is unbearable to her ego to think of him absorbed in the cocoon of his adult preoccupations: ' "What in the name of all that feels, has he to do with *books*, when I am dying?" ' She reacts with childish pique to his apparent safety from her tantrums. But at the same time, she responds with a deeper childlikeness of spirit which relates her both to her own orphaned childhood and to the child who is yet to be derived from her, Cathy. The challenge to her power is the catalyst that starts off the 'childish diversion' with the pillow, accompanied by a speech that echoes Ophelia's in her madness in Shakespeare's *Hamlet*, but which turns the reader's imagination progressively out of doors— away from books, rooms, the confined space of the present moment, into the immensity of the external world of the heath and of Heathcliff:

> "That's a turkey's," she murmured to herself; "and this is a wild-duck's; and this is a pigeon's. Ah, they put pigeon's feathers in the pillows—no wonder I couldn't die! Let me take care to throw it on the floor when I lie down. And here is a moorcock's; and this—I should know it among a thousand—it's a lapwing's. Bonny bird; wheeling over our heads in the middle of the moor. It wanted to get to its nest, for the clouds touched the swells, and it felt rain coming. This feather was picked up from the heath, the bird was not shot— we saw its nest in the winter, full of little skeletons. Heathcliff set a trap over it, and the old ones dare not come. I made him promise he'd never shoot a lapwing, after that, and he didn't. Yes, here are more! Did he shoot my lapwings, Nelly? Are they red, any of them? Let me look."

All this while, Catherine is removing feathers from her pillow and sorting them. As she sorts them, she names them. As she names them, she relates them to her own destiny. There is a language of flowers, trees, birds and animals which has still not died out. It is related to that folk-lore legend for which, given its tough, enduring roots in her inheritance, Emily Brontë had a tenacious memory.

Each bird Catherine names springs into life in our imaginations from the bits of feather which are its sole mortal remains, taken by human hands from the carcass of a bird known to us both for its own beauty as a natural creature and for its traditional meaning and suggestions. The domesticated turkey gives way to the wild duck which is an emblem of freedom but hunted by man. Then the Yorkshire superstition that pigeon's feathers restrain the human spirit from passing out of the body is supplied by Catherine as an explanation of why she cannot 'burst the fetters' of her condition by willing death so intensely. The pigeon is gregarious, tame, obedient, associated with domesticity and the 'homing' instinct that binds her to Thrushcross Grange: she is bound to a continuing and unwanted life in a social order in which she is expected to act the wife's part, that tame, unspirited profession. The moorcock leads out beyond the range of the domestic world in which she is suffocating. Outside all this is the lapwing nesting upon the upland heath, in some shallow exposed basin of the earth, rearing its young at the mercy of every intruder. The lapwing and its baby birds are an exact emblem of Catherine's nature and her plight.

Catherine speaks as if in a waking dream, of a place in which she will never again be a presence; nor is the lapwing at that moment a presence. It is mid-winter, and the lapwings have probably migrated. Male lapwings return to choose the site of a breeding-ground in mid-February or March: by that time, when Linton brings her the wild golden crocuses Catherine will be dying. She is within this 'shattered prison', her body, enclosed within that other prison of Edgar's house, in extremity, and engaged in the 'baby-work' of undoing the stuffing of a pillow, the symbol of all the warmth and comfort that pads and dulls her existence at Thrushcross Grange. Someone has made this pillow, the paranoid's 'they'; some enemy to the person she is. She takes what 'they' have fabricated to pieces and restructures it; traces the finished (dead) product back to its living sources. Birds have died to make the pillow on which she is meant to lay her head. In the pillow many species' feathers are anarchically mingled: muddle, chaos, is revealed as the basis of the pillow—that, and cruelty too, for much killing of beautiful natural creatures had to be done in order to make up the pillow. Catherine reveals in this most poignant moment that the civilized world, priding itself on its rationality, mildness and gentle behaviour (Edgar reading in his library) depends on exploitation. She pulls out the inside and analyses it down into its unthinkable reality. Her will is to undo it all: unweave the mess that poses as order and remake the lives on which it preyed. The urge is to return to source. The task, like Psyche's, is not in any way viable unless the riddle can be solved, the code broken, which explains the system in which we all grow. There is a strong sense that this passage is making some emotional and philosophical assault on us with which we are called upon to come to terms. The likelihood is that we respond to the unanswerable by turning with Nelly to the safe haven of a request to 'Give over with that baby-work'.

But as we move out in imagination on to the heath where the single lapwing swerves and rides the air currents, turning for its nest, we also move back in time, to a single occasion before that great loss of Heathcliff which cut through Catherine's life like a physical bereavement. The piteous image of the nest in the 'middle of the moor', seen in winter by the two children 'full of little skeletons' is a central symbol within *Wuthering Heights*. We later gather that Catherine, speaking this memory to Nelly, who has decided not to comprehend it, is pregnant. She speaks, in a tradition known in Yorkshire, of the moorland bird as a symbol of the soul liberated from the body, or wandering the earth yearning for heaven. One of Emily Brontë's profoundest affinities is with the wild birds who are almost the sole living inhabitants of the moors. She had observed their habits and behaviour, and studied the natural science of Bewick's *History of British Birds*, painstakingly copying out in minute detail the engravings there. *Wuthering Heights* bears the fruit of this knowledge. Like humankind, the bird-life of the novel speaks of a search for liberty, soaring between the mountains; like our race, their fertility is burdened with seasonal change, the cruelty that is within nature, the high mortality-rate which took such a toll in Emily's own life and which in her art she both expressed realistically and tried to heal in the course of a mythic, cyclical structure. *Wuthering Heights*, in the person of Catherine, tells of a world which is a mighty orphanage, in which at best we are fostered for a limited period, on sufferance. But equally through the person of Catherine, it suggests the process through which we may guess at the existence of kin, seek them out, bond and mate with them, whether on this side of the grave or on the other. And so the birds of Catherine's reverie symbolize her predicament, and suggest its universal nature. The lapwing is near relation of the golden plover whose overhead whistling has, in a northern legend, been associated with the doomed Jews, wandering eternally after the crucifixion; the plaintive curlew's low-pitched fluting was associated in the north with the 'Seven Whistlers', portending death. Emily Brontë is able to harness the power of these ancient legends of birds whose inhuman music calls like an agent of destiny into the human world. Yet the creatures Catherine lists are also felt as real, living and warm presences, linked to people not just as messengers but because they are so like us. The lapwing especially is known by its behaviour-patterns as a parent-bird. Its 'pee-weet' note extends when its young are in danger to an acutely distressful call, uttered in tumbling flight. The parent-birds feign to be crippled or to drag a wing in order to draw off danger from the exposed nest. The woman who looks back on the outing to the moors where she and Heathcliff were most at home sees an image of beauty—'Bonny bird'; freedom 'wheeling over our heads', shot through with menace, inexhaustible longing for home which belongs equally to human and to animal nature, as an instinct rather than a decision. Catherine imagines the bird as having freely moulted the feather she has picked out of her pillow, but the bird was as subject to vicissitude as she now is, pathetic in its longing as she will be in a few minutes, lying back on the much-criticized pillows, 'her face bathed in tears ... our fiery Catherine was no better than a wailing child!' The lapwing is like her in being a parent, with the elements gathering against her: rain is coming. In the midst of its soaring flight it is a prisoner, like Catherine, dashing for home before calamity can strike. Catherine is five months pregnant: she is herself a nest from which the future will derive. Yet her image is of that time after the breeding-season in which (winter then as now) she and Heathcliff were out again and saw the nest 'full of little skeletons'. This desolating vision of a small family of forms bereaved at their very inception, yet held cocooned in the circle of the nest, their home become a tomb open to the winter skies, is an image for what Catherine feels she holds within her, fertility that is blighted because it comes of Linton. Equally it is an emblem of her own childhood, orphaned like this, exposed in a family of two with Heathcliff after the death of her father and protector, to the enmity and indifference of an uncaring sky.

We always are, in Emily's mythology, the child we were. At the very centre of the novel, in the protracted death of Catherine, the birth of Cathy, this truth is affirmed and reaffirmed. In looking at that nest, barred with a trap, with its starved, exposed little skeletons, we remember that terrible first grief of Catherine as a child:

> The poor thing discovered her loss directly—she screamed out—
> "Oh, he's dead, Heathcliff! he's dead!"
> And they both set up a heart-breaking cry. I joined my wail to theirs, loud and bitter . . .

The only adult present, Joseph, somewhat less than true to the vigorous spirit of the departed, and utterly, satirically unmoved by the grief of the orphans that remain, lets forth a blast of chilling moral air by wanting to know 'what we could be thinking of to roar in that way over a saint in Heaven'. In their mutual shock and grief, Catherine and Heathcliff become one with the narrator, Nelly: their loss is hers, and the infuriating Catherine with her naughty ways, her petulance and her need, becomes for Nelly 'the poor thing'. Catherine, after so many times teasing her father till he was moved to say the unthinkable ' "Nay, Cathy . . . I cannot love thee" ', had come on the last evening of his life to lay her head quietly against him; Heathcliff's young head pillowed on her lap; moved to kiss him goodnight, put her arms round his neck and found him dead. Nelly cannot get to the children in their grief. She looks in through their bedroom door late that night and sees that:

> The little souls were comforting each other with better thoughts than I could have hit on; no parson in the world ever pictured Heaven so beautifully as they did, in their innocent talk . . .

We have been allowed to see a nest of little orphans, cut off for ever from the parent who was their only guarantee of shelter. They are exposed to the rancorous humours of Joseph; the jealousies of Hindley; the intermittent mothering that Nelly can or will give.

Our minds touch upon that memory when we read of the dead lapwing chicks in their nest on the moors, cradled in their grave. What Catherine remembers of that vision of the dead young birds carries for us another painful acknowledgement. It was Heathcliff who in his young, unmitigated cruelty, set the trap that introduced the fledglings so early to their mortality. Catherine starts looking for evidence of blood upon the feathers she has pulled from the pillow. Heathcliff, whom she has said she does not love but rather *is*—like a part of her own identity, a force of her own nature—is implicated in the cruelties of the human and the natural world. Later in the novel he will 'lay the trap' over the nest of the child Hareton and his own son, Linton Heathcliff, degrading the one and tormenting the other without any hint of remorse. The 'little soul' whom Nelly watched with awe in his bereavement communing with Catherine suffers only to cause more suffering. In her poetry, Emily Brontë had constantly reverted to the theme of a rejected child handicapped throughout life because of rough early conditions,

> bred the mate of care,
> The foster-child of sore distress.

Pain begets cruelty; rejection unkindness, reciprocally, so that we act as transmitters down the generations of the wrongs that are done us. It is less a case of original sin than of original pain. That is why Emily Brontë everywhere insists on universal forgiveness for all offences whatever. Seeing through the walls of the adult self to the defenceless child each person contains, it is not thinkable to cast the first stone. Catherine recognizes Heathcliff's 'fierce, pitiless, wolfish' nature: ' "he'd crush you, like a sparrow's egg, Isabella" '. He is the barbarous cruelty of the heath itself, with its lowering weather; the wild part of Catherine's own nature which she had thought to have tamed, but also the victim of that pattern with which Emily was so personally familiar, whereby the world is a system for orphaning the young; bringing to destitution; killing mothers; undoing twins; betraying affinities. Heathcliff, who is the agent of so much destruction in *Wuthering Heights,* is as automatically an innocent as any being born into such a system.

At the very centre of the whole novel, Catherine suffers, dies and gives birth. If we take a radius from that point, we encompass the whole novel, so that the structure is a perfect circle. Like the great myths of antiquity, *Wuthering Heights* presents us not only with a story of rebirth but also with a myth of return. The narrative at once presses forward and doubles back to its source. From the first Hareton Earnshaw who built the Heights in 1500, we are brought to the last Hareton Earnshaw, who restores the ancient line. Though the novel is precisely timed and documented to the year, the day, the hour, almost to a fault, and the very first word is a date (1801), the forward push of heredity and causality, with its vigilant eye on the clock, is retarded by a process of recapitulation. From Catherine's speech about the lapwings, we can move to almost any other point in this great prose poem and find some echo or resonance. Devices such as repetition and recapitulation of places, persons, events, names, and even of the letters which begin those names—the mysterious 'H's of Hindley, Hareton, Heathcliff, suggestive of a family cluster of improbable likenesses, and even a provocative code which tempts us to try and break it—reinforce this sense of a circling reality. Lockwood's narrative encircles Nelly's, which in turn encircles other stories told in their own persons by Zillah, Catherine, Isabella, Heathcliff, in letters, or retold dreams, or simply verbally. The beginning echoes in the end; the end in the beginning. Fractionally before the mathematical centre (so perfectly is the whole novel balanced), the elder Catherine dies and the younger is born; yet the dead Catherine is felt by a reader as just as strong and living a presence in the second half as her daughter and namesake. In the cross-breedings of the two families, the mild Lintons and the harsher Earnshaws, washed through and renewed by fresh blood, there is a sense of something fated and inevitable. The personalities of the characters, though so odd and eccentric, come to seem, in this inexplicable pattern of return to source, as impersonal as their setting, the wind that is busy on the moors and the abeyance of self that is under the moors.

The novel is not so much about individuals as about humanity. It is less about humanity than humanity in a setting. It is far less about humanity in the person of the male of our species ('man', 'forefathers', 'God the father', 'masterpiece') as about humanity in the person of the female. The author of *Genesis*, looking back to our origins, had felt called upon to attribute to Adam a sort of womb where his rib-cage was, by biological sleight and to the confounding of commonsense, deriving woman from man. For a person as radical as Emily Brontë, and innocent of the offence her perceptions might cause the vulnerable minds of the orthodox, writing of the theme of genesis, this would simply not seem sensible, credible or even efficient according to the laws of practical economy. She expresses instead a female vision of genesis, expulsion and rebirth in terms of the metaphor of fertility and childbirth. Wordsworth and the Romantic poets, whom she deeply admired, had taken the imagination back to childhood, to muse over the idea of the child as 'father of the man', a metaphor for our beginnings. Emily Brontë, in a way that is radical and difficult because no language has existed in patriarchal England to express it (foremothers, mistress piece, God the mother?), relived the idea according to the more natural metaphor of the child as mother of the woman. Catherine's mothering of Cathy at the centre of the book relates past to present; projects present into future, so that past and future meet at source. The ethic of this feminine way of encountering reality is that of universal forgiveness; the metaphysic is one of final but mysterious redemption; the means of expression is that of a coded, secret utterance which, though we feel we understand fully while we read, has the knack akin to that of dream-language of slipping just out of comprehension when we awaken.

Toward the centre of *Wuthering Heights* occurs the transition where past meets future, youth meets age, death meets life. It is very like the structure of Shakespeare's tragi-comedies: 'thou mettest with things dying, I with things new born', where, through the channel of labour from which a living girl-baby is drawn from the birth-canal of her dying mother we are led to brood upon the deepest mysteries of human existence: a living cycle which includes and transcends individual deaths and mortal-seeming bereavements. Emily Brontë starts Chapter II of Part II with a characteristic telling of the time: 'About twelve o'clock, that night, was born the Catherine you saw at Wuthering Heights . . .'. She directs us to the moment of transition, the crucial turning point at which the threshold between two worlds is doubly crossed. The baby Catherine has come in; the mother Catherine's soul crosses with that of her child, on its way out. Twelve o'clock is the mid-point, at which the old day has given place to the new. All is grief and loss in this new day: the baby who has come in seems not, yet, to count. Nelly describes the aspect of

Catherine lying dead as a scene of peace, but we do not always trust Nelly's evaluations, suspecting her of sentimentality at some times, as of vinegar sourness at others. Yet when she describes the moment of Catherine's departure to Heathcliff outside, there is a sense of perfect truthfulness:

> "How did she die?" . . .
> "Quietly as a lamb . . . she drew a sigh, and stretched herself, like a child reviving, and sinking again to sleep; and five minutes after I felt one little pulse at her heart, and nothing more."

Nelly is filling in information for Heathcliff, her head turned from Lockwood. She opens a window for us, into the immediate past, through which we have a chance of apprehending Catherine's last moments in this world. Emily Brontë constantly reveals just as tender and naturalistic an observation of the gestures and behaviour of babies and children as of the moorland creatures whose nature she knew by heart. If you have seen a little girl in a deep sleep, coming gently to the surface, perhaps roused by some dream, and then relapsing downward into the inner world without breaking the surface of consciousness, then you have seen Catherine's death as Emily Brontë meant you to imagine it. A child observed in sleep is poignant, existing in a remote world: to us who watch her, helpless, to herself unaware of being vulnerable, beyond the need for help. Nelly transmits an image of the soundest peace, in which the hearer may draw comfort as if from a well. In her telling, death has lost its sting; the grave its victory. She speaks of Catherine 'sighing'. A sigh which normally speaks to us of pain, is presented as the breath of life, prelude to 'revival'. We feel that Catherine does revive in some other world. The child goes home. Nelly touches Catherine's breast; records the final sign of life, 'one little pulse'. Her tenderness for this woman whom she has not much liked is shown quickened as Catherine, who has just borne a child, herself becomes one. As her daughter wakes into this world, we are given to believe that the mother wakens into another, as she had predicted and as Nelly feels constrained to echo: 'Incomparably beyond and above you all'. Nelly reinforces the idea of regression to childhood as the way out of the imprisoning mortal condition by going on to say that ' "her latest ideas wandered back to pleasant early days." ' The mighty circle of *Wuthering Heights,* in which the Hareton Earnshaw who built the Heights in 1500 returns to the Hareton Earnshaw who will marry this new young Cathy on 1st January, 1803, is informed by smaller circles, leading us to muse on the final and original identity of 'late' and 'early'; first and last; mother and daughter. There is no linear path from present into the future, as if the world were laid out flat as a map; the map, Emily Brontë everywhere tells us, is a useful fiction which must not be mistaken for the shape of reality. In moving forward over the round world we recapitulate our mutual and personal history. Thus Nelly speaks of Catherine's 'latest' thoughts (the last things) as 'wandering back' to 'early days' (her source and birth). To 'wander' suggests those rambles on the moors which offered prospects of Paradise to Catherine and Heathcliff, together with freedom from adult authority; to 'wander' in mind means to go mad; to 'wander back' means the joy of retracing steps without deliberate purpose but with the sure instinct of homing birds— like the pigeons Catherine has been seen feeding; of whose feathers in the stuffing of her pillow she had bitterly complained as keeping her soul hampered in the flesh. We are reminded too of Catherine's hallucination, when, going out of her mind at the onset of her illness, she had lost seven years of her life:

> I did not recall that they had been at all. I was a child; my father was just buried, and my misery arose from the separation that Hindley had ordered between me and Heathcliff—I was laid alone, for the first time . . .

In her delirium, Catherine had not managed to 'wander back' far enough into childhood, but fell back only to the moment of exile which is a source of her present pain, confirmed by her own voluntary betrayal of Heathcliff for Linton at the age of 17. That return landed her in a sudden, inexplicable liaison with a 'stranger; an exile, and outcast'. Her wandering mind could do no more than settle her at the crucial moment of loss.

For Emily Brontë, the adult self is felt as a stray fragment of a greater whole, of which we may intensely dream or hallucinate, but not recover until we meet as children at our starting-point. For the elder Catherine, Heathcliff is this whole; for the younger, it will be Hareton to whom she goes home by some true instinct bred perhaps of the Linton tempering of her constitution, of her mother's mortal suffering, and of some maternal-seeming destiny suggested but never explained by the novel. In a last, deep relaxation of her fretful being, Catherine is shown by Nelly as being able to shed the years and be the child she was. In her poetry, Emily had many times implied this possibility. Near the eve of her coming-of-age, she speaks of the damp evening landscape 'breathing of other years':

> Oh, I'm gone back to the days of youth,
> I am a child once more.

In an undated but probably late poem, she expressed the myth of going back which Catherine enacts in her dying moments, in a metaphor of going out on the moors which also includes the idea of wandering in mind:

> Often rebuked, yet always back returning
>   To those first feelings that were born with me,
> And leaving busy chase of wealth and learning
>   For idle dreams of things which cannot be . . .
>
> I'll walk where my own nature would be leading:
>   It vexes me to choose another guide:
> Where the gray flocks in ferny glens are feeding;
>   Where the wild wind blows on the mountain side.
>
> What have these lonely mountains worth revealing?
>   More glory and more grief than I can tell:
> The earth which wakes *one* human heart to feeling
>   Can centre both the worlds of Heaven and Hell.

Here the poet dramatizes the regressive process which she sees as the key to the sources of creativity and value by inverting the grammar: 'turning back' becomes 'back returning'. 'Often' is resisted by 'always'; 'rebuked' superseded by 'return'. In *Wuthering Heights*, Nelly enacts the adult world's 'rebuke' of the child consciousness in man, which constantly performs an abrupt about-turn and goes sprinting back for home in accordance with the laws of its 'own nature': ' "Give over with that baby-work! . . . Lie down and shut your eyes, you're wandering. There's a mess!" ' Nelly spends most of her time expostulating as the lawless child-heroes give her the slip; wander off on the moors; push each other around; play serious games. To her infuriated demand that they grow up, they reply by silently eluding her grasp (as the second Cathy will do, by a stealth foreign to her guileless nature, to reach the Heights), and circling back to their starting-places. Heathcliff finally resists the onward pressure of time to move into the future by starving himself to death, until, 'washed by rain', with his hand grazed upon the open window, and his unclosable dead eyes staring into the mortal world as his living eyes had gazed into the immortal one, he is placed with Catherine in the one grave. They sleep together. Over his grave, Hareton 'with a streaming face' weeps like a child, not in proportion to the usage he received from the 'sarcastic, savage' corpse he is burying, but according to the laws of his own strong and loving nature, and because he finds himself in some way kin to the foster-father who abused him. Hareton is true to his childhood roots; Heathcliff returns to his, as the author holds we do return, not in a 'second childhood' of senility, but first childhood, where we began.

Heathcliff himself, the destroyer, vengeful, avaricious, lying and sadistic as he is, remains (especially at the moment of his most abject loss, in the centre of the book) profoundly and organically in touch with this process of recreation. He was the cuckoo in the nest who disturbed the world of the Heights, and outraged its symmetry of brother and sister balancing brother and sister at Thrushcross, whose intermarriage might in the course of things have taken place. He was the bane of Hindley and will be the potential undoing of Hareton. The only creation we can attribute to him is his sickly, spineless and degenerate son, Linton Heathcliff, sired on Isabella in a fit of hate. Yet Heathcliff is associated by Emily Brontë with a kind of harmony and fertility which underlie all the other levels of order and disorder that superimpose in complex strata in the novel. Beneath the immaculate and fastidious social order symbolized by Thrushcross Grange and the Lintons' way of life, Catherine has discerned a predatory disorder, through her 'baby-work' of undoing the pillow. At a yet deeper level, beneath the disharmony of Catherine's early death and Heathcliff's huge, inexplicable loss, is revealed a buried principle of a benign though pagan shaping-out of a destiny that is ultimately fruitful and kind. Emily Brontë allows us to glimpse this mysterious reparation which lies at the core of loss, through the most delicate allusions to the relationship

beween man and his natural setting, especially birds and trees.
Nelly describes his appearance as she approaches him with the
news of Catherine's death:

> He was there—at least a few yards further in the park;
> leant against an old ash tree, his hat off, and his hair soaked
> with the dew that had gathered on the budded branches, and
> fell pattering round him. He had been standing a long time in
> that position, for I saw a pair of ousels passing and repassing
> scarcely three feet from him, busy in building their nest, and
> regarding his proximity no more than that of a piece of
> timber. They flew off at my approach, and he raised his eyes
> and spoke:
> "She's dead!" he said.

It is spring. The buds of the ash in March are large and sticky;
here they are covered in early-morning dew which overflows them
on to the bare head of the oblivious watcher beneath, keeping
vigil. The ash is old, having seen many seasons. Heathcliff is felt to
be deeply related to the surge of new life in the old stock,
inevitably, subconsciously so. In Nelly's description, he seems to
belong to the landscape as an intrinsic part of it—as if he were
planted there, rooted not as a human and active entity but as a
different species, quiet as the trees with which he is surrounded.
He is recognized as a harmless part of nature by the inhabitants of
the natural world going about their business—the ring ousels
building their nest, who are not afraid to come within three feet of
his stock-still body because they are ignorant that he is human
and their natural enemy. They recognize Nelly sure enough, and
depart. The ring ousels are emblems of fertility; in their pairing
and nest-building they speak to us of the future. Emily Brontë will
have known that this is a species in which both sexes build the
nest, incubate and tend the brood; that they are related to the
thrush (appropriate, then, to Thrushcross), and are reckless in
protecting their young from predators. We remember the nest of
little skeleton chicks over which Catherine mourned, and perhaps
look forward to the later image of her daughter Cathy as a 'bird
flying back to a plundered nest which it had left brim-ful of
chirping young ones'. Heathcliff is a force causing such
destruction to the young, yet here at the centre of the novel he
seems to be imitating an opposite role. The ousels have returned
early to their familiar nesting-site to build from the coarse grasses

which they are conveying across Heathcliff's line of vision. We are
directed to the moment at the very turn of the year. Indoors the
baby is new in its crib; the breeding birds are in a pair outside,
building for the future. In this scene, the mateless Heathcliff—
outside the human community, alongside these emblems of
fidelity, the homing instinct, protectiveness, warmth—stands
spiritless as 'a piece of timber'. Contrary to his own intentions,
and against his will to destroy and uproot, he is in deep harmony
with the scene, even a contributor to it.

In the second half of the novel, Heathcliff tries to thwart and
mutilate the products of this fertility. Yet toward the end, it
becomes clear that he cannot destroy anything; that he is in a
strange way the agent of a harmony for which he cannot wish. Far
from thieving the property of the Heights and the Grange from
their rightful owners, his efforts marry the two inheritances by
bringing the two heirs into proximity. The 'little dark thing,
harboured by a good man to his bane' as Nelly muses, is not
ultimately a 'bane' at all, but an instrument of regeneration and of
harmonious balance between eternal oppositions. *Wuthering
Heights* hinges on a fruitful but—in rational terms—baffling
paradox: order and disorder, creation and destruction, being born
and dying, looking in and seeing out, enclose and define each
other, as if in a series of multiple parentheses. Within this pattern
Heathcliff, for all his efficient manipulations, is caught static. He
is, at the centre, a 'piece of timber', rooted in the seasonal cycle, at
whose foot the breeding birds are free to fulfil their instinctual
nature. At the end of his career he is again static, ceasing to act
because his cycle is fully lived out:

> I have to remind myself to breathe—almost to remind my
> heart to beat! And it is like bending back a stiff spring . . . it is
> by compulsion that I do the slightest act not prompted by one
> thought, and by compulsion that I notice anything alive or
> dead, which is not associated with one universal idea. . . .

Under his very eyes, Hareton (' "the ghost of my immortal
love" ') and Cathy, who are in some respects so like himself and
Catherine in their earlier lives, but tempered, reshaped and
reshaping, are moving toward each other, to mate and build.
Heathcliff is in process of turning back into the bedrock earth from
whose rough nature he seems made: heath and cliff. Emily Brontë
suggests a mode of existence intermediate between 'human' and

'nature', in which the subconscious continuum of our living—to breathe with our lungs, to pump the blood round with the heart— is coming to a deliberate standstill. Heathcliff, to stay alive at all, has to make a mental labour of the unthinking processes of survival. It is all said in the brilliant image of 'bending back a stiff spring': incarnate existence has become to him a matter of mechanics predetermined to tend in an undesired direction. Nelly stresses in these latter moments of Heathcliff's life that he really does not seem quite human. But all she can suggest to explain him is that he might be a 'goblin' or a 'ghoul, or a vampire'. She knows this to be very feeble and embarrassing when she reflects that she 'had tended him in infancy', the vampire species having no known childhood. Joseph is much happier with his explanation when he shuffles in to view the corpse, announcing with malevolent joy that ' "Th' divil's harried off his soul" '. There is a beautifully wry note in Nelly's description of Joseph as 'the old sinner', as he grins back at his master's face set in rigor mortis, and, labelling him a fiend, looks ready to dance for joy all round the death-bed. When Heathcliff is buried, Nelly feels anxious that he bears no surname, simply the one (surely not a 'Christian') name, which is inscribed simply and singly upon his gravestone. Heathcliff has moved from a death-in-life to a life-in-death with Catherine. He has passed through the window; reverted, as Gimmerton Kirk will do, to the moor. Personality is annulled, but a new, impersonal, more absolutely vital existence is felt to begin as the heath which is his original claims its namesake.

At the centre, Nelly, having seen Catherine on her passage out of the world and Cathy on her way in, enters the park expecting that Heathcliff had been out 'among the larches' all night. It is characteristic of the author to name the species of tree rather than to refer to generalized trees. The larch is a fir but not ever-green, shedding needles annually from delicate, slender boughs and with the spring reclothing itself in soft pale-green. Mid-way between the evergreen and deciduous worlds, it looks like the one, behaves like the other. Heathcliff is absorbed in his waiting into the wood. He beats his head against the trunk of the ash in his agony: "I observed several splashes of blood about the bark of the tree, and his hand and forehead were both stained; probably the scene I witnessed was a repetition of others enacted during the night." This extreme behaviour has often been seen as a bizarre intrusion of Gothic in which the obligatory maniac behaves like a howling beast rather than a man. But there is a deeper, mythic meaning to these actions. Heathcliff now has a double nature: he both lives and does not live. Catherine, who is conceived of as his own being, will be buried and he left above ground, 'with his soul in the grave'. In this absolute loss he meets the boundaries of human nature but cannot get across. Nelly sees him as an animal. It is easier for her to formulate the idea of the non-human in these terms. The breeding birds see him as a tree. We see his blood shed upon the bark of the ash and staining it; his forehead too is stained with blood as if baptismally. In the image of the blood-stained tree Emily Brontë suggests an analogy to the sacrificial slaughter either of animal or man, by which the ancient mystery religions sought to appease the deities and ensure a fruitful new year. Heathcliff's pain is absolutely acute. The year, the hour, the day turn; the baby is born, the birds mate. The old mother passes, while the man's blood, like that of the sacrificial king of ancient pagan religions, seeps into mother earth.

The happiness of the future, Emily Brontë asserts, is built on the destruction of the past, and is seen by the reader to depend on it. In one of the most poignantly beautiful images of *Wuthering Heights*, stated matter-of-factly two chapters later, Nelly says of the second Catherine, whose birth had killed her mother: 'For the rest, after the first six months, she grew like a larch; and could walk and talk too, in her own way, before the heath blossomed a second time over Mrs Linton's dust.' 'Six months' takes us to September, the year's turning into winter: Cathy has it in her to resist and overcome winter. Since the moorland heather blooms in August to September, the same sentence takes us through yet another full cycle, placing an image of hope and renewal (the purple bells of heather) directly upon an image of loss and mortality (Mrs Linton reduced to 'dust'). The child has in her the best of the Lintons and the best of the Earnshaws, in fruitful mixture. If she is 'like' her mother she is also 'like' Heathcliff, since we must believe Catherine's conviction that 'I *am* Heathcliff'. As he stood in the terrible night of Cathy's birth amongst the larches, and shed his blood upon the bark of a tree, so Cathy 'grew like a larch'. In some mysterious way, Heathcliff is intrinsically linked to the second Cathy, and has given up some of his life to her.

7 In at the Window

Rites of Passage

WHEN the principle narrator of *Wuthering Heights*, Lockwood, has to spend the night at the Heights, he is led in to a room which in its turn contains a smaller room. This is the clothes-press in which the elder Catherine had slept as a child. To get in, he has to slide away the side-panel. Inside this womb- or tomb-like place, he finds a window, upon whose ledge are a few old, mildewed books, and the three scratched names—*Catherine Earnshaw, Catherine Heathcliff, Catherine Linton*. Lockwood is a constitutional voyeur; he cannot help climbing in and peering round at other people's business. In telling the story, he provides the framed window of his mind in order that we too can scrutinize certain secret places. Lockwood himself is glad of the privacy of the press, feeling 'secure against the vigilance of Heathcliff, and everyone else'. This is not surprising in view of the fact that, in attempting a get-away from the unwelcoming inhabitants of the Heights, he has just been set on by 'two hairy monsters' named as the dogs Gnasher and Wolf, causing him to emit an outburst of choice and unexpected oaths, and an undignified nose-bleed, to the amusement of his host. Lockwood feels so sorely ill-used that he is able to compare himself in his sufferings with no less a person than King Lear on the heath.

The architecture of the dead Catherine's bedroom, with its window-within-a-room-within-a-room, and Lockwood peering about inside, is like a parable of the conception of reality which the novel enacts. Reality for Emily Brontë is intricately relativistic. She raises the familiar premise that life is a mesh of anecdotes, which can be related on the 'I said to her and she said to me' principle, to the status of a philosophical system. The author never tells you what to think, or how to interpret the material which comes filtered through so many people's inset dreams, anecdotes, letters, hieroglyphs, diaries, snatches of song, reminiscences, inscriptions on houses and signposts. You have to draw deductions as you do in life itself, whose riddles and clues no

114

authority can conclusively solve, and it is just to be hoped that you will be a little less idiotic than Lockwood, rather less sententious than Nelly, in coming to your conclusions. *Wuthering Heights* rudely mocks its reader. Equally it haunts her or him. Like the bits of diary which Lockwood is able to decipher in the press, Emily Brontë does not offer her book as a fictitious means of bridging the gap between present and past: she reclaims only fragments, leaving us to guess or dream the rest, so that we feel the presence of the elder Catherine's childhood and of her survival after death with the most vivid certainty, yet are not given the slightest conclusive evidence for that survival. Lockwood as a 'reader' of these experiences is not so different from ourselves reading and trying to make sense of the fragments he pieces together, despite the fact that we are encouraged to laugh at him. With his vision framed by his own inadequacies, which are legion, Lockwood (trying to get further and further in to the true story of the Heights) only has access to a framed reality, and cannot know what to call interior, and what exterior—appearance or reality— since every 'inside' place seems to enclose and therefore be displaced upsettingly by yet another 'inside'. For within the closet are books. Inside the books is the elder Catherine's fragmentary diary, scrawled down the margins of the New Testament. This is Catherine's own testament, like a window into the past through which we can glimpse only odd views and catch scraps of conversation (as in Emily's and Anne's own diary-papers). Worryingly, there seem to be three Catherines, each with a different surname: the 'characters'—a fruitful pun suggesting both individuals and handwriting—are baffling, and seem maliciously capable of raising spectres, for when Lockwood nods off the air seems to swarm with Catherines, and he jerks hurriedly awake. By the end of the novel we have solved the riddle of the three Catherines, Earnshaw marrying Linton, begetting a Linton who will marry a Heathcliff, but by the end we have travelled on to a last and first Catherine: the younger Cathy who in a new testament returns to the old in marrying an Earnshaw. The cycle is riddling and confusing, even when we know the answer.

Being in the press causes Lockwood to dream; he sees a ghost, as if to validate Heathcliff's conviction that Catherine haunts him. The press where Catherine slept as a little girl and which seems the deeply innermost interior place connects organically, by the window, with the widest outside. Its sliding panel prefigures the panel of the tomb which Heathcliff will bribe the sexton to remove so that when he is buried he may come to her. The press in which Lockwood gets such a fright is supernaturally arousing to the most commonplace of men because it represents, as in some extraordinary conundrum in modern physics, the point of intersection between inside and outside. For Lockwood, it links the past with the present, for Heathcliff the living with the dead There is, of course, a perfectly naturalistic explanation for Heathcliff's conviction that Catherine is still a living presence beyond the grave. The recently bereaved do feel their dead brush past them, as if they laid aside the air as they moved invisibly in some adjacent world. They sense their eyes upon them or hear them breathe. This must be the common feeling which prompted human nature from the remotest past to credit the walking of ghosts, the possibility of thresholds in special places and at certain momentous times, through which we might enter—nerved to the highest pitch of our natures—to join the dead, or be joined. Emily Brontë's subject is what makes our hair stand on end and is also the function of one of our most poignant desires: to edge up to the imagined border between the seen and unseen worlds, and both to see and to travel through. Her symbol of the window mediates this passage. Heathcliff, taking Lockwood's place at the lattice, calls through it:

> "Come in! Come in!" he sobbed. "Cathy, do come. Oh do—
> *once* more. Oh! my heart's darling, hear me *this* time—
> Catherine, at last!"

The intensely stressed rhythms of Heathcliff's pleading to the thin air of the world outside the window to release its hold of Catherine to him qualify this speech as a kind of poem. Yet Lockwood says that he 'sobbed' the words; he is a child again, and cries. At these moments of heightened nervous stimulation when the soul reaches beyond the mortal, personality regresses into its infancy, where the borders between 'self' and 'other', I and you, were not known to be so unyieldingly hard. At these points, standing at the window, nothing of what Heathcliff has done or will do matters at all. As at the moment of birth, and as at the graveside, moral problems and attribution of guilt are stilled: there is original and final innocence.

Emily Brontë records this innocence. The idea that her novel is 'immoral' or 'amoral', or inconsistently moral, comes of an irrelevant perspective. Standing with her characters at the window between mortal and immortal where—as in her poems—our dying clay is shown as able to take 'fresh root in Eternity', she introduces us to the personal innocence which, as it was there when people were originated, is reborn in their final form. The Gondal poems are alive with this theme, stripping the layers of behaviour off the central core of innocence by which in the final analysis all must be judged. In a poem of 1838, written when she was nearly twenty, she expressed it very simply:

> If thou hast sinned in this world of care,
> 'Twas but the dust of thy drear abode—
> Thy soul was pure when it entered here,
> And pure it will go again to God.

The following year she writes of a harsh, dark man, sullenly at odds with a soft spring scene, who obviously prefigures Heathcliff both in his nature and in the standards of judgement she applies:

> That iron man was born like me,
> And he was once an ardent boy:
> He must have felt in infancy
> The glory of a summer sky.

To be an 'iron man' is to seem derived from another element than the delicate human tissue which is sensitive to inner warm feelings ('ardent') and to outer sunlight. The poem muses, as does *Wuthering Heights,* on how it is that people of such cold metal might have come to lose their memory of early tenderness, under the influence of storm, so as to reject a world which rejects them. The speaker reflects that this morosely Byronic or Satanic character now at variance with man and nature had once reached a 'tiny hand' to bring flowers to 'weave' into his mother's hair. Weaving and twining suggest in Emily Brontë's work the harmony of a deep communion, as with the hair of Catherine, Linton and Heathcliff which is woven together in the dead woman's locket. The poem wonders how we become disconnected from this mingling of childhood with the mothering earth and the effects of the nurture given by a human mother. The moral imperative deduced from this thought is that the unforgiving must be forgiven: to be 'born

like me' is an adequate moral qualification for acceptance.
Heathcliff is the supreme example of a being disconnected from
his natural source, found orphaned on the streets of Liverpool
without mother-country or recognizable mother-tongue, but
'born like me'.

Only very heretical Christian sects like the Gnostics have
believed that all, including the Serpent who tempted us, merit
forgiveness, and that we slough our sin along with the incarnation
which coats us in it. Emily Brontë in the detached tone in which
she narrates Heathcliff's lurid crimes is such a heretic. She holds
nothing of his behaviour against him when he comes up to the
window and calls through it. There is a stern moral clarity and
kindness in this view. Both Emily's sisters disliked the Christian
concept of Hell, suggesting as it does God's inhumanity to man, so
that Anne could write of a hope on which her whole spiritual
happiness depended that 'even the wicked shall at last/Be fitted
for the skies'. Emily Brontë registers this view in a more
commanding and provocative, powerfully visualized manner, as
character after character approaches the window to look and call
through. At the centre of the book, Catherine in her delirium gets
the window of her bedroom at Thrushcross Grange open,
oblivious to the harm in the icy air, and looks over toward the
Heights at another imagined window where she thinks Joseph is
waiting up for her with the light on. She has said, ' "I wish I were
out of doors—I wish I were a girl again, half savage and hardy,
and free" '. Her longing to regain the freedom of her spartan
girlhood will require for its fulfilment a new sort of hardihood,
courage to go underground, into the churchyard itself:

> "It's a rough journey, and a sad heart to travel it; and we
> must pass by Gimmerton Kirk, to go that journey! We've
> braved its ghosts often together, and dared each other to
> stand among the graves and ask them to come ... But
> Heathcliff, if I dare you now, will you venture? If you do, I'll
> keep you. I'll not lie there by myself; they may bury me
> twelve feet deep, and throw the church down over me, but I
> won't rest till you are with me ... I never will!"

Catherine is preparing to return to sleep with Heathcliff, healing
their separation. There is no question that she will seek or find
final restoration of harmony in the Church, in which the only

thing to interest her seems to be the churchyard ghosts with whom she and Heathcliff played childish games of 'dare-devil', calling up the ghosts as Heathcliff at the window of the Heights will call for her. This final, grown-up 'dare' involves such a flouting of the institution of the Church that it looks forward to the ultimate destruction of that sacred edifice, which will be reduced in Catherine's fantasy to the heap of dead stones for bricking up the human spirit which it really is. Her threat to slip across the borders of the dead world to haunt the living until the congregation of the conventional is scared out of its wits to such a degree as to be willing to ' "throw the church down over me" ', conveys not only the relish of the illicit which is so strong in Catherine's character but also what seems a powerful contempt entertained by the author for the institution of the church itself. It offers no window into the other world. The sanctimoniousness of a religion which revels in the conviction that we are all grovelling worms (with one or two named exceptions, the Elect) is forcefully parodied in the rasping person of Joseph through the novel. The dead body of received orthodox religion is dramatized in the building of Gimmerton Kirk. As Emily Brontë was writing, she could see the Church of St Michael and All Angels from her window; it was her father's church, and the church of her fathers. Inside this unhealthy edifice, the decomposing dead endured underfoot, aromatically present to the nostrils of the congregation. It was an area of deliberate darkness and breathless air, where the injunctions not to sin; the nasty consequences of sin; the doctrine of our bad beginnings, our errant journey and our sorry end were reiterated every Sunday. Patrick Brontë, a benevolent and philanthropic Christian, did not emphasize the roasting-in-retribution aspect of his faith more than any parson of sound Anglican views must do. Nevertheless, Emily, detecting it as the foundation of his excellent principles, appears to have abandoned it, increasingly abstaining from church attendance. In *Wuthering Heights*, struggling for a grounding in the next world and arrived at the limits of this, Catherine sardonically rejects the Church as anything more than the sum of its raw materials. The genuine spirit may bring its weighty ballast of stone down upon itself without sustaining the least shock. There is a feeling that Catherine's movement toward a spiritual vision of 'that glorious world' which is beyond matter altogether, begins in an iconoclasm that refuses to be intimidated by repressive dogmas enshrined in a sepulchral building.

Whenever we see Gimmerton Church in *Wuthering Heights,* it has crumbled a stage further into decay, until at the very end of the novel Lockwood visits it to discover the trinity of graves in the churchyard at the moor's edge:

> When beneath its walls, I perceived decay had made progress, even in seven months—many a window showed black gaps deprived of glass; and slates jutted off, here and there, beyond the right line of the roof, to be gradually worked off in coming autumn storms.

Catherine's 'dare' seems to be in process of being fulfilled; 'they' are pushing the church down on the churchyard through neglecting it. There is no 'window' in the building worth looking out of or into, only a number of black gaps like sightless eyes. There is something altogether positive in the idea of decay 'making progress': the progress will be complete when Gimmerton Kirk has reverted entirely to the moor, its roof unslated to let in the sky, its structure consigned to that phase of the pastoral cycle which comes with 'autumn storms', spelling good riddance to the obsolete products of the old year and making way for a fresh spring. Lockwood comments casually that this demolition of the sacred architecture by nature had gone ahead very efficiently in 'seven months'. We remember that the younger Cathy, the hope for the future, had been born a premature 'seven months child'—about the earliest prematurity in which there lay hope of survival in those days of high infant mortality. 'Seven' is a magical number in all traditions, signifying death with the implicit possibility of rebirth. Cathy had been born out of the 'shattered prison' of the elder Catherine. The natural world, to which Emily Brontë transfers the sacramental power and virtue conventionally associated with the Church, usurps the rubble of the old dispensation. The death of the church is a movement towards spiritual liberty, a reclamation of that 'principle of life, intense,/Lost to mortality' which is to be found in the fresh air outside our forefathers' religion. To see the church fall back into the earth from which it was forged, emptied of inmates like a liberated Bastille, is to see the consummation of a kind of labour on the part of nature: Lockwood observes that autumn storms will work off' the slates, as if bringing a successful enterprise to completion. The window will then be open for the whole sky to enter. This is the product of a heresy which expressed itself two years before Emily Brontë's death in 'No coward soul', through the conception of a 'God within my breast', which is more heretical than that of any of her Romantic predecessors except the atheist, Shelley:

> Vain are the thousand creeds
> That move men's hearts, unutterably vain,
> Worthless as withered weeds
> Or idlest froth amid the boundless main
>
> To waken doubt in one
> Holding so fast by thy infinity
> So surely anchored on
> The steadfast rock of Immortality
>
> With wide-embracing love
> Thy spirit animates eternal years
> Pervades, and broods above,
> Changes, sustains, dissolves, creates and rears
>
> Though Earth and moon were gone
> And suns and universes ceased to be
> And thou wert left alone
> Every Existence would exist in thee
>
> There is not room for Death
> Nor atom that his might could render void
> Since thou art Being and Breath
> And what thou art may never be destroyed.

Catherine's ' "I won't rest" ' is in harmony with the poet's celebration of the divine as energy, recognizing no boundaries in its unpunctuated movement between dimensions. As a creator-spirit, it 'broods', pensive as the contemplative mind and fertile as the mother bird incubating the future; 'rearing' its young to have high minds. Pride is not seen as a sin. This spirit links eternity to time in that it 'changes'; to love because it 'embraces' and 'sustains'; to ecstasy in its 'dissolving' of barriers, and to acceptance of apparent mortality because 'dissolution' and 'dissolving' are cognate. By comparison with this energy, dogmatic religions seem vanity, as a kind of froth on somebody's consciousness. Like Blake, Emily Brontë has obtained release from the 'mind-forged manacles' of slavery to Christian orthodoxy.

Similarly, while Edgar Linton is off worshipping the God of his forefathers at Gimmerton Kirk, Catherine and Heathcliff in their final meeting are desecrating the Sabbath, by a climactic affirmation of their mutual bond. She is spoken of as sitting, very quietly, 'in the recess of the open window', looking round abstractedly. Nelly is careful to describe the way that her hair, having been shorn during her illness, lies very short around her face and neck, and that she is clothed 'in a loose, white dress'. Presumably it is 'loose', because she is advanced in pregnancy. But its whiteness, and the cropped hair, suggest an initiation, signalling the rite of passage toward which the novel has tended, the double transition from one state to another, in which the baby is to be born and the spirit of the mother to take its leave. Catherine at the window is a neophyte prepared for change. The final meeting is the conscious violation of a taboo, a sacrament celebrated through the communion of two spirits in vehement contradiction of the church service which is going on simultaneously. The mood and situation have something in common with the primitive paganism of the old Danish and Scottish ballads on which Emily had fed her imagination as a child. Heathcliff's three-year absence has been left unexplained like the seven-year gap in the grim ballad 'The Daemon Lover', in which the suitor returning to claim possession of his bride finds her appropriated by a new husband:

> 'O where have you been, my long, long love,
>   This seven years and mair?'
> 'O I'm come to seek my former vows
>   Ye granted me before.'

Heathcliff resembles the 'long, long love' who returns to find Catherine Earnshaw equipped with a new surname. In the ballad the lover persuades the wife to abandon her husband and two babies, sailing away in his ship whose sails are of 'taffetie', masts of 'beaten gold'. Heathcliff too has come back handsomely dressed, fit to kill:

They had not saild a league, a league,
    A league but barely three,
When she espied his cloven foot,
    And she wept right bitterlie.

'O hold your tongue of your weeping,' says he,
    'Of your weeping now let me be;
I will show you how the lilies grow
    On the banks of Italy.'

He shows her the hills of heaven 'Where you will never win' and the mountain of hell 'Where you and I will go'. Finally, swollen to a colossus of Satanic power, he sinks her and the ship in the sea.

Emily Brontë had brooded with relish on the idea of demonic possession as a metaphor for a mental process. In 'I'll come when thou art saddest', written at the age of 19, the voice of some daemon intruder promises to manifest himself:

> my influence o'er thee stealing,
> Grief deepening, joy congealing,
> Shall bear thy soul away.

But Emily Brontë's poem and her novel accept this violent intrusion as fundamentally desirable and creative, though not necessarily sought-after. The ballad-wife who is seduced into adulterous elopement is understandably appalled at viewing the beloved's 'cloven foot'; presumably aghast at the prospect of Hell he holds out; and less than elated at her abrupt capsize. The ballad, sinister as it is, enshrines an age-old patriarchal moral: that no good will come to women who forsake their legal bondage. Emily's version contradicts this moral. Awareness of this reinforces our sense of how vitally she writes as a woman, who gives no automatic credit to men's laws, institutions and religions. Catherine meets her daemon with fierce longing and with open eyes as the ballad-wife does not. Where the latter is desolated at the loss of Heaven, Catherine was never in doubt as to the location of her true spiritual home, neither wanting nor intending to enter the Christian Heaven. As a girl of seventeen, she tells Nelly of a dream in which:

> heaven did not seem to be my home; and I broke my heart with weeping to come back to earth; and the angels were so angry that they flung me out, into the middle of the heath at Wuthering Heights; where I woke sobbing for joy.

It is immediately upon overhearing this speech that Heathcliff leaves, after which Catherine may be said to have silently broken her heart with weeping in the meek and mild Heaven of the Linton household. It would be only grounds for complacency in Catherine to discover that 'you will never win' the hill of Heaven but rather the mountain of Hell, if that would mean unity with her alter ego, on the uplands where Wuthering Heights is situated. The movement of her longing is to the centre, the source: 'the middle of the heath'. At the centre, surrounded, there is both safety and freedom. Her idea of a Heaven where angels are so intemperate that if you rub them up the wrong way they become angry and reject you is a criticism of a paradox (or a hypocrisy, depending on your point of view) that stands at the heart of Christian dogma: the ruthless 'Justice' that underlies the smiling 'Mercy' of Christian ethics. 'Angry' angels belong logically in Hell, not Heaven. It is also an allusion to, and a verbal echo of, the repeated theme in *Wuthering Heights* of the rejection of young children by their parents or foster-parents. When the child, Heathcliff first comes to the Heights, 'Mrs Earnshaw was ready to fling it out of doors', and Nelly 'put it on the landing of the stairs, hoping it might be gone on the morrow'. Hindley's manic passion for his son Hareton is in itself a form of rejection:

> "Hush, child, hush! well then, it is my darling! wisht, dry thy eyes—there's a joy; kiss me; what! it won't? Kiss me, Hareton! Damn thee, kiss me! By God, as if I would rear such a monster! As sure as I'm living, I'll break the brat's neck."

Again, the child is an 'it', an alien thing to be possessed; fondling is coercion; the melody of Hindley's intended lullaby deteriorates into a bellowing rant of vituperation. This initial rejection of children by the world into which they fall by being born, is shown by Emily Brontë as threatening to warp and degrade. Even the adored second Cathy comes into the world unwanted by her mother, unnoticed by her father, wished out of existence and also out of gender by her nurse, Nelly (for as a girl she will not inherit): 'An unwelcomed infant it was, poor thing! It might have wailed out of life, and nobody cared a morsel, during those first hours of existence'. For Nelly, Cathy on arrival is a 'thing', an 'it'. Nobody's arms are willing to embrace her. The angels are angry, and eager to fling intruders back into the darkness from which they have struggled. *Wuthering Heights,* like Blake's *Songs of Experience,* echoes with the sound of children's inconsolable crying.

It is in the context of a world in which fellow human beings, whether lovers, parents, brothers, retainers, friends, are liable to turn around and reject you that the affinity between Catherine and Heathcliff, the union of like with like, becomes sacramental. The place where they have been most fully able to enjoy the freedom to be themselves, the moors, equally takes on a sacramental meaning. It is a sanctuary, pure of humanity, and a playground where no repressive adults scrutinized the games Catherine and Heathcliff enjoyed as children. Their games are holy to them; their night-wanderings represent the active enjoyment of their mutual security. It is this identity of twinned solitudes which leads Catherine to the extravagance of her statement that ' "I *am* Heathcliff" '; her sense that their natures are shaped from the same elements, fire or lightning, by contrast to Linton's cool surfaces, his mild light. From this derives her agreement with Heathcliff that her marriage was a sacrilege, betraying her own truest nature. Catherine and Heathcliff are envisaged as the twin halves of a single being; their final meeting is an attempt to heal the division by force, so that they can return to the sacramental safety of their early days, unmaking and purging their adult selves and bridging the many occasions of separation, misunderstanding and disloyalty which accumulate between childhood and maturity.

The final effort at union, so often said by readers to be asexual and 'purely spiritual' is described and made vivid in terms profoundly suggestive of physical passion. No Victorian author ever made the sexual element more explicit. Edgar is sitting quietly in church with his mind on higher things while Heathcliff speaks to Edgar's wife through the medium of flesh and blood rather than words:

> He neither spoke, nor loosed his hold, for some five minutes, during which period he bestowed more kisses than ever he gave in his life before, I dare say, but then my mistress had kissed him first. . . .

Nelly, to mediate any torrid elements, goes so far as to time the kisses and to comment with laconic irony upon the mathematics of Heathcliff's previous endeavours in the way of kissing. But the

bathos of her ' "I dare say" ' only intensifies our sense of the
privacy of that passionate silence. Nelly later remarks on the blue
impression of his fingers on Catherine's pale, wasted arms, where
he has roughly bruised her. Later again, Catherine 'made a
spring, and he caught her'. . .

> she put up her hand to clasp his neck, and bring her cheek to
> his, as he held her: while he, in return, covering her with
> frantic caresses, said wildly . . .

While the speeches are expressive of spiritual yearning rather
than sensual desire, the narrative elucidates a language of the
body in terms of which the actors in this ritual communicate.
There is no ambiguity about the sexual association of the phrase
'covering . . . with frantic caresses': Emily Brontë could not more
clearly or less puritanically have declared the conviction that
body and soul share the one nature. What Heathcliff goes on to
say, after the poignant moment of Catherine's drawing down his
head to hers, continuously responds and replies to her physical
presence and actions:

> "You teach me now how cruel you've been—cruel and false.
> *Why* did you despise me? *Why* did you betray your own heart,
> Cathy? I have not one word of comfort—you deserve this.
> You have killed yourself. Yes, you may kiss me and cry; and
> wring out my kisses and tears. They'll blight you—they'll
> damn you. You loved me—then what *right* had you to leave
> me? What right—answer me—for the poor fancy you felt for
> Linton? Because misery, and degradation, and death, and
> nothing that God or Satan could inflict would have parted us,
> *you*, of your own will, did it . . ."

This torrent of accusations is accompanied by physical responses
to Catherine's actions, for she is imagined to be kissing him and
weeping as he speaks, and he replies in kind, ' "Yes, you may kiss
me and cry . . ." '. It is also a statement of a moral code; a
redefinition of the principles of right and wrong in terms of the law
of their own natures, moving toward an assertion of the
relationship between a private and mutual code of values and the
classifications that prevail socially and spiritually in the orthodox
Christian world. Heathcliff is accusing Catherine of an act of
betrayal amounting, according to this code, to apostasy. It is the

unforgivable sin for which he judges her. His words are a curse. Catherine acknowledges the sin by confessing that ' "I'm dying for it" '. In his love, Heathcliff rejects her as an outcast, reprobated and exiled to a condition of damnation. These emotive words from Christianity—the doctrine of sin, judgment and retribution—come naturally from Heathcliff. He and Catherine used to hear this kind of thing night and day from Joseph at the Heights, presiding over their childhood bawling (according to Catherine's diary), ' "shame on ye! sit ye dahn, ill childer!' ", and that ' "owd Nick" ' would come and fetch them as his own.

Emily Brontë parodies the Christian game of counting sins in Lockwood's dream of Jabes Branderham's unspeakable discourse on the text 'Seventy Times Seven'—'good God! what a sermon: divided into *four hundred and ninety* parts . . . and each discussing a separate sin!', and the violent squabble as to who had sinned the 491st (unforgivable) sin—whether Lockwood for mutinying against the preposterous sermon, or Jabes himself, for presuming to bore the congregation to death. But Catherine and Heathcliff have assimilated this doctrine of election and damnation to their own anti-Christian religion, whose God is themselves as a single unit of being; whose church is the moorland; whose enemies are pain, human and social animosity, mortality, and 'God and Satan' both. This is the blasphemy which lies at the root of their cult. God and Satan are viewed as more or less identical enemies, with nothing to choose between them, impotent and irrelevant. Power lies with Catherine but she has betrayed it: Heathcliff accuses her of the unforgivable sin against their faith, the sin that exceeds the 'Seventy Times Seven'. But Emily's allusion in Lockwood's ridiculous dream is to a part of the Bible which concerns not judgment but compassion. The original text in Matthew 18:22 narrates Christ's answer to Peter's enquiry as to whether it would be adequate to forgive his enemy if he had sinned, say, up to a total of seven times against him:

> Jesus saith unto him, I say not unto thee, Until seven times: but, Until seventy times seven.

Christ clearly did not envisage the future existence of characters of such superhuman arithmetical virtuosity as Joseph or Jabes who would be able to keep a tally on the quantity of sins committed, forgive the lot up to 490, and then pounce. Christ's meaning is that we forgive all sins whatever; that absolution is universal and unlimited. This beautiful doctrine—which is Emily Brontë's overwhelming conviction, and her sole concession to Christianity—occurs in the same chapter in which Christ, having been asked who was greatest in the kingdom of heaven, called to him a little child to stand as a parable for all who elbow and jostle for position in the mistaken earthly hierarchy:

> Take heed that ye despise not one of these little ones; for I say unto you, That in heaven their angels do always behold the face of my Father which is in heaven.

In *Wuthering Heights,* Emily Brontë shows a hell on earth which prevails as children are despised; the children's creation of a new heaven and a new earth in the light of their own radiant perceptions. The vision moves toward forgiveness and reconciliation, partially in the first generation, wholly in the second. To Catherine's ' "I forgive you. Forgive me" ', Heathcliff can reply, ' "I forgive what you have done to me" ', and they 'wash' each other's faces with their mutual tears. This rinsing by tears, an ancient symbol of absolution, but—realistically—wrung from them in despair at the threshold of parting, is the final phase of their rite of passage, from the old world into the new. Linton returns; Heathcliff removes himself. Between the first and second chapters of the second volume Catherine dies.

8   *This Lamb of Yours*

The Triple Bond

TOGETHER, Catherine and Heathcliff have taunted Edgar
Linton for being effeminate, in the ugly manner of a gang of
children whose safety in numbers makes it possible to stigmatize
an outsider without fear of reprisal. The author plainly shows the
hateful, anti-social side of the child-in-man, against which even,
or especially, a civilized adult stands disadvantaged, burdened
by his moral reflexes. These two grown-up children are not
inhibited by any inconvenient standards of decency. First they
conspire to goad Linton into losing self-control:

> Heathcliff measured the height and breadth of the speaker
> with an eye full of derision.
> "Cathy, this lamb of yours threatens like a bull!" he said.
> "It is in danger of splitting its skull against my knuckles. By
> God, Mr Linton, I'm mortally sorry that you are not worth
> knocking down!"

Linton's slight stature, fair complexion and habitually gentle
temperament are rooted in the fertile and protected valley in
which Thrushcross Grange is built. The relative opulence of the
Grange and its parklands, which had so turned the young girl
Catherine's head by arraying it in a 'feathered beaver' and fitting
her up in silks, has confirmed the inbred Linton tendency to
pleasantness, courtesy and respectability, which Catherine and
Heathcliff find easy to label unmanly. Their target is so bad at
being aggressive that he can emit only the most pompous noises
when he tries to be, and can act forcibly only when goaded to the
quick or in the company of armed retainers. Heathcliff
witheringly sizes up Linton's slender body (which Catherine had
so loved) and sneers at the pet-lamb, supposedly the mere
property of Catherine, whose slightest contact with Heathcliff's
clenched fist would smash its frail skull. Incapable even of
wrestling with his wife for the key to his own house:

> Mr Edgar was taken with a nervous trembling . . . He leant
> on the back of a chair, and covered his face.

"Oh! Heavens! In old days this would win you knighthood!" exclaimed Mrs Linton. "We are vanquished! we are vanquished! Heathcliff would as soon lift a finger at you as the king would march his army against a colony of mice. Cheer up, you sha'n't be hurt! Your type is not a lamb, it's a sucking leveret."

The two tormenters try out a range of tame or insignificant creatures with a view to identifying the species of animal they are goading. Lamb and mouse give way to the 'sucking leveret' of the unweaned mother's-boy. Catherine mockingly invokes the laws of chivalry which forbid a contest with a weakling of such sub-human dimensions, according to the code of courtly love in which a husband must in honour challenge a suitor. Lockwood had described himself, in the illness to which he succumbs in Linton's study long after the latter's death, and before he knows the story at all, as being 'feeble as a kitten'. Comparison with Lockwood, who at his only recorded contact with a woman bolted into his shell 'like a snail' at the first sign of response is unfortunate. It is also invited by the hieroglyphic chime of names, according to which we experience the savage trinity of Hindley–Heathcliff–Hareton opposing the mild and civilized pairing of Linton–Lockwood.

But Lockwood, the outsider, only travesties Linton. Where Linton is warm, Lockwood is cold; where the one is kind, genuine and loyal, the other is facile and mannered. We are not asked or expected by the author to sympathize with the infantile callousness of Catherine's and Heathcliff's provocation of Linton, whose loneliness increasingly draws our concern. The 'lamb's' nature is belied suddenly, as he strikes and winds Heathcliff; as for the 'sucking leveret', perhaps we remember Emily Brontë's poem 'Well, some may hate', in which it is asked:

> Do I despise the timid deer
> Because his limbs are fleet with fear? . . .
> Or hear with joy the leveret's cry
> Because it cannot bravely die?

Even if Catherine's slander were a truth, no contempt could be merited. The animal images which link Catherine and Heathcliff to creatures of prey—as wolf, as carrion bird—and Linton to victim—lamb, mouse, hare—are as deceptive and complex as any other aspect of the novel. Seeming so powerful, Catherine is only responding out of the weakness of her divided nature; Heathcliff's brutal remarks are generated by the useless emotion of envy; and Linton's status as victim is an illusion, for his tormentors are also his victims. This undermining of the expected power-relationships is introduced early in the novel, when Edgar, having been treated to a first unedifying sight of Catherine having a full-scale tantrum, goes off in shock:

> The soft thing looked askance through the window—he possessed the power to depart, as much as a cat possesses the power to leave a mouse half killed or a bird half eaten—
>
> Ah, I thought, there will be no saving him—He's doomed, and flies to his fate.

Linton is being seduced by Catherine's tears, so that the 'soft thing' with his 'dove's eyes', his 'lamb's' nature, would be expected to stand in the role of victim in the relationship. But this double emblem shows his departure as being arrested by a carnivorous hunger, whose appeasement must be fatal for the partner. It is Catherine's life which hangs in the balance here, not that of the soft feline predator, the romantic lover; she who will be torn between the loving power of a husband, and the need for her first love. She will die of Linton. The application of this 'Darwinian' image of power in human relationships, suggesting a possible collusion between passive sufferer and active agent, the power that lies in docility and the infirmity which may flaw a strong nature, emphasizes the complexity of the novel's conception and structure. You are required to take nothing for granted.

The two opposed principles which are the dynamic source of the novel's action are personalized in the Lintons at Thrushcross opposing the Earnshaws (including Heathcliff) at the Heights. These principles are generally thought of in meteorological terms, as 'storm' and 'calm'. In *Wuthering Heights,* the attachment of opposites is likely to come to grief, though its product—if it is bred of love—may fuse and reconcile these variations. In the features of the second Cathy's face are coded the imprint of both kinds of personality which made possible her kind of being. Nelly spells out for the reader the meanings of that face, the implications of its temperament:

a real beauty in face—with the Earnshaws' handsome dark eyes, but the Lintons' fair skin, and small features, and yellow curling hair. Her spirit was high, though not rough, and qualified by a heart sensitive and lively to excess in its affections. That capacity for intense attachments reminded me of her mother; still she did not resemble her; for she could be soft and mild as a dove, and she had a gentle voice, and pensive expression: her anger was never furious; her love never fierce; it was deep and tender.

The grammar of this face and disposition is all composed of balancing qualifications: 'but . . . though not . . . still'. Whatever Cathy 'is' balances with what she 'is not'. Nelly describes the Earnshaw traits, stressing the reflection from mother to child in the look of the eyes, the tenacity of the affections, but grateful to be able to list the 'Linton' part of the inheritance, which cancels out (for Nelly) the unlovable attributes of the Earnshaw contribution. But Nelly's 'reading' of Cathy may be partial, for according to her the Linton chromosomes are so dominant as to carry the field before them with no trouble. The Cathy we learn to know is not quite the 'dove' Nelly hatches here, but a bird more free, with intuitions corresponding to her mother's so closely that she is drawn constantly to enquire back to the part of her which 'lies on the other side' of Penistone Crags. She wants to be told the name of 'those golden rocks'. Nelly replies by taking the gloss off them:

> I explained that they were bare masses of stone, with hardly enough earth in their clefts to nourish a stunted tree.

In reducing Penistone to as prosaic and boring an image as she can manage, Nelly tells nothing but the truth. The sunlight is a charming fiction; the beauty of the rocks rests in their simplicity as 'bare masses', their unyielding affirmation of their own architecture, without elaboration. Nelly wants to make them as uninspiring as possible to the little girl, in order that she may remain quiet and safe within her father's house. Yet as Nelly delivers this discouragingly plain description, she paradoxically activates the 'Earnshaw' character in Cathy: attempting to retard the gene provokes it out of its recessive state. As readers we are also activated and provoked, for in that unemotive description Nelly has accidentally struck against the beauty of those 'eternal rocks beneath' which the unfolding story has through many repetitions made instinct with feeling and mystery. But this time the bare words 'rock', 'stone', 'flint', 'slate', 'whinstone'—even 'barren wilderness'—have taken into themselves an extraordinary energy or magnetism, like that of the mysterious stone circles of prehistoric times. Like Cathy we want to shed the Edenic safety of Thrushcross and move again outward toward the Heights, gladly setting aside the Linton part of ourselves, with its kindly comfort, because as Cathy says ' "I know the park, and I don't know those." ' She is eager to eat the fruit of knowledge. Yet the rocks are by definition unknowable: Nelly says they are unclimbable, which is the same thing. The beauty which 'rock' has accrued depends on its representing a mystery, or *the* mystery, on which however intently we ponder (with Cathy's 'pensive' expression, her father's reading habit) we cannot break or decipher. The impenetrable rocks, centralising the novel, draw an unslaked curiosity which they will never satisfy or let fall. They are the catalyst for the rousing of the 'Earnshaw' element in Cathy against the Linton.

More deeply, the 'Linton' and the 'Earnshaw' principles are recognized as essential to one another. Edgar Linton and Catherine Earnshaw are seen as naturally drawn to one another, and happy in enjoyment of one another's company during Heathcliff's three-year absence. Thrushcross Grange and Wuthering Heights seem equally necessary to one another, whether there is commerce between them or not, like the poles of one world, the variables of a single personality. Wholehearted choice between the two on the part of a reader is not really possible: like the characters, we fluctuate, veer, or are held in painful (at the end, gentler) tension between them. On some occasions we choose against the open-air freshness of the Heights, with its cruel, capricious or attenuated personalities, dwelling with relief on the scope offered by Edgar Linton for a way of life that is tolerant, sensitive, and brave enough to hold the male conventions of mindless violence espoused by most of the dwellers at the Heights in the contempt they deserve. Additionally, Linton shares the best qualities of the Earnshaw nature, for his attachment to Catherine bears exact likeness to Heathcliff's, despite the latter's offensive remarks to the effect that you might as well plant an oak in a flower-pot as expect her to flourish under his tender care. As Heathcliff's love is durable and intense, so also is Linton's; it covers her life-time, and the entire remainder of his. Linton's 'raised eyes, that seemed dilating with ecstasy' on his death-bed at the thought of final union with the beloved seen through the veil of their daughter Cathy's features, and his insistence on being buried with her at the limit of the graveyard, outside the vault of his ancestors, testify to a commitment as absolute as Heathcliff's. The author never denies, though Heathcliff and Catherine herself may, that Linton will enjoy such a final union with Catherine, though against the bias of her mortal self. Heathcliff speaks slightingly of Linton's mere 'humanity', but this does not mean that either author, reader or narrator is deceived into giving a genuinely humane nature less than its due. Linton is a true father where Heathcliff is not, and the only parent in the novel consistently to behave to his child in a natural way.

Emily Brontë does not, however, rest here, nor invite the reader to recline on any assumptions or prejudices which would interrupt the constant flow and agitation of the mind striving to embrace apparently opposite principles. Subtly, a Linton temperament (even when it is not perverted into a Linton Heathcliff) contains unsavoury elements which may be outlived and outgrown but never entirely forgotten. The boy Heathcliff tells of the children's first view of the Linton offspring through the window of the Grange, hooting with laughter at the sight of Isabella Linton, aged 11, in full tantrum at one end of the room, Edgar grizzling to himself by the hearth, and a pet dog which they had nearly dismembered in a squabble over possession stranded on a table voicing its misery. Heathcliff, who might be expected to detest the lucky and pusillanimous boy, seems more astonished than anything, not by the Linton violence which is his own second nature, but by the sense of a wasted privacy and privilege. His indictment of the Linton children to Nelly is a moral one:

> "When would you catch me wishing to have what Catherine wanted? or find us by ourselves seeking entertainment in yelling, and sobbing, and rolling on the ground, divided by the whole room?"

We share the product of the trespasser Heathcliff's spying-activities in the Linton garden; sharing forbidden knowledge. The boy's imagination is awed at the waste of time and space represented by the Lintons' behaviour. He satirizes their activity of 'yelling, and sobbing, and rolling' as though this were a deliberate policy for passing the time, and, viewing with him from the outside, we sympathize with his condemnation of such demented behaviour. Loving Catherine as himself, and looking on physical closeness as an almost holy obligation, Heathcliff's shock at the state of frivolous civil war in the Linton household has something like a religious dimension. To be 'divided by the whole room' when a private room means the availability of union unimpeded by tyrannous adults appears to the child like a violation of a taboo. The 'outside' children make frightful noises at the window to terrify the 'inside' children who have bolted to the door wailing ' "Oh, mamma, mamma! Oh, papa! ..." '. It is a parody of the manners of civilized mothers' darlings who are only brats at heart, comparable to Joseph's later jeerings at Isabella's affected utterance: ' "Mim! mim! mim! ... Minching un' munching! Hah can Aw tell whet ye say?" '. Heathcliff speaks against the Linton vices of spinelessness and property-mindedness; their abuse of a sanctuary by using it as a dividing-space. An inner room is for Heathcliff the watcher a private place, a single mind. An innocence speaks through him, exposed and rejected as he is ('an out-and-outer', says the servant who catches him), an innocence unknown to the lucky, protected children within. Their life-style gives itself away to the voyeur's eye as that of cruel weaklings, protected by their aptly-named bull-dog Skulker in pulling their lapdog in two. The author shows the potential closeness of weakness and cruelty. In Heathcliff's eyes, the Lintons betray their own childhood (it is tantamount, in *Wuthering Heights*, to betraying your class) and through their failure to do the honourable thing of ganging up against the adults, carry a stigma of dishonour. If it is true to say that *Wuthering Heights* is structured on the pull of opposites, Lintons and Earnshaws, it is more exactly true that each opposite itself contains something of its own opposite: the so-called 'children of calm' contain a latent violence, while the 'children of storm' can be tender and gentle. It is a complexity which outstrips definition.

Emily Brontë's conception of character does not incline to the view that we come pre-formed into the world, so that the role of time is simply to unwrap the package. As the firs and hawthorns at the Heights grow 'all one way' because of the prevailing north wind, so human character is planted in a landscape whose conditions help to determine its tendencies. Images sent up by the novel at crucial moments even suggest that character is or can become a kind of landscape, to which we may respond or belong as we do to certain kinds of scenery. As Heathcliff is embittered, isolated and demeaned in the course of his adolescence, so as to seem a poor creature in the eyes of Catherine in her newly-acquired finery and tastes, so the character of Linton softens and grows mellow and receptive:

> Doubtless Catherine marked the difference between her friends as one came in, and the other went out. The contrast resembled what you see in exchanging a bleak, hilly, coal country for a beautiful fertile valley; and his voice and greeting were as opposite as his aspect—He had a sweet, low manner of speaking, and pronounced his words as you do: that's less gruff than we talk here, and softer.

It cannot reflect well on Linton that his accent is associated with that of Lockwood, with his milk-and-water temperament, nor to be assimilated to the idea of a southerner, anything south of Liverpool lying well off the relevant map. Yet the unfolding beauty of Linton's person as he grows toward manhood is powerfully evoked by Nelly's description of him as 'a beautiful fertile valley'. Archetypally, this is an image of the feminine—receptive, cupped, soft and maternally green. The 'bleak, hilly, coal country' impersonated by Heathcliff is an emblem of the male. His black hair and eyes suggest the black of coal, with an implication of a hidden mineral resource deep beneath the surface. Yet these two opposite sorts of personality are oddly dependent on one another. We only see Linton so clearly because of the relief in which he stands against Heathcliff; as the 'one came in . . . the other went out'. The comely face and ways of Linton are expressed in the observer's mind as a reflex of the glowering, unlovely and profoundly suffering Heathcliff. The landscape metaphor is an organic one, embracing both natures in terms of a single world, in which opposite kinds of country are the conditions of one another's existence. Though Linton is the only genuinely 'fertile' man in *Wuthering Heights*, the metaphor suggests that in a mysterious or riddling way Heathcliff is the complement that makes such fertility possible. As male is to female, so Heathcliff is to Linton. On the one, nothing can take root and flourish, but its barren, monumental forms automatically shelter the richly yielding nature of the other. They are mutually necessary.

Ignoring the usual conventions of gender-classification as matters of little relevance, Emily Brontë had not bothered to make the kind of revolutionary 'feminist' protests which her sisters both expressed in their novels about the sexual stereotyping which limited women's lives to an affair of darning socks, looking decorative, keeping quiet and getting married. To make such a protest would have resembled visiting an asylum to denounce the madness of the inmates. *Wuthering Heights* is concerned with those aspects of human nature which cross the border of gender and are the groundwork of our humanity: this is how Catherine can claim to '*be*' Heathcliff, with a love that stresses kinship and affinity, the sense of a beloved human being as an extension of oneself, the notion with which we are haunted that the sexually beloved is a kind of 'double', reflecting and completing us. Yet the novelist does make use of traditional images of 'feminine' and 'masculine' natures, to structure and set forth the poles of our experience, the dynamic oppositions within human nature and nature itself: the 'beautiful fertile valley' against the 'hilly coal country'. Women, however, are not necessarily 'feminine' predominantly, men not 'masculine'. Lintons have, broadly speaking, the former kind of character, Earnshaws the latter. When Charlotte Brontë came to defend her sister's novel after Emily's death against charges of excessive harshness, she hit obliquely upon this problem:

> For a specimen of true benevolence and homely fidelity, look at the character of Nelly Dean; for an example of constancy and tenderness, remark that of Edgar Linton. (Some people will think these qualities do not shine so well incarnate in a man as they would do in a woman, but Ellis Bell could never be brought to comprehend this notion: nothing moved her more than any insinuation that the faithfulness and clemency, the long-suffering and loving-kindness which are esteemed virtues in the daughters of Eve become foibles in the sons of Adam. She held that mercy and forgiveness are the divinest attributes of the Great Being who made both man and woman, and that what clothes the Godhead in glory, can disgrace no form of feeble humanity.)

Though Charlotte seeks to smooth out the vital eccentricities which roughened her sister's work, we seem to catch in the phrase 'nothing moved her more . . .' an authentic echo of Emily's anger at the thought of male gentleness being labelled weakness. Sifting through the characters in *Wuthering Heights* for soothing examples of 'feminine' natures, with a view to making the novel seem morally more acceptable, Charlotte has to make do with one of the narrators, and with a man. This creates for her a fresh set of problems.

The idea of *Wuthering Heights* had gone through Emily Brontë as Catherine's dream through her system, 'like wine through water': her vision is coloured in a way that Charlotte's Preface does not begin to comprehend. Emily knew that what she set forth would probably not be understood save by those through whose mental world it washed like a dream remembered on first waking, when all one's faculties seem charged by an altered awareness. Nelly as good as says so to Lockwood; and Lockwood innocently passes the sarcastic probe to us, to make what we like of it. Nelly has been moralizing, quite boringly, on what a God-fearing and therefore satisfactory man Edgar Linton was in time of calamity. Then she breaks the thread to observe:

> But you'll not want to hear my moralising, Mr Lockwood: you'll judge as well as I can, all these things; at least, you'll think you will, and that's the same.

Nelly recognizes, wryly, the extent to which we are sealed within the capsule of our own bias, like seeds which will not grow. The message from author to reader is a shrugging invitation to us to make what we like of it. It is all one to her if the reader cannot budge from her or his complacency, because the radical story endures irrespective of our assumptions. Catherine in her 'baby-work' tore the stuffing of the pillows at the Grange to shreds: the author vaguely threatens us that if we really unsealed the self to confront the story as it is, something painfully like this might happen to us. The outer narrator is blandly mocked by the inner; the reader of a potentially revolutionary novel is mocked by the author.

This unsettling moment occurs at the point at which Nelly has been telling of the growth of Edgar Linton's love for his daughter. His way of loving has been described as deeply 'maternal' rather

than 'paternal' in character. Nelly speaks of the role adopted by
Linton to Catherine during her illness:

> No mother could have nursed an only child more
> devotedly than Edgar nursed her. Day and night he was
> watching, and patiently enduring all the annoyances that
> irritable nerves and a shaken reason could inflict. . . .

Linton, just as uncritically as Heathcliff, is devoted to a single
dominating passion, to such a degree as to be impervious to any
violation of the social norm into which this might lead him. Emily
Brontë could have alluded to 'fatherly' care without losing all the
sense of commitment in the image, but she chooses not to: Nelly
carefully associates Linton with a 'mother' sitting up with her
young child night after night, not as something extraordinary for
which praise and gratitude might be due but as a supposedly
instinctive and thankless role. There is an extra dimension to this
role because Edgar is being motherly to a 'child' who is herself an
expectant mother containing his own child. Again, the large
enclosing structure of the novel, with its complex series of
containments, is being echoed within a single detail. Edgar in his
passion has crossed the 'normal' threshold of gender—easily and
without fuss, since it is in his nature to do so, abdicating in his
extreme love the male status which he had so flimsily maintained
and so little liked at the best of times. His apparent desertion to the
'feminine' which so many ignorant men might scorn, represents
for Emily Brontë an absconding in the direction of a radical kind
of virtue, a quieter heroism. In outwardly taking on the 'feminine'
role and potentially opening himself to male sneers, Edgar
expresses a fortitude and single-minded stoicism such as his
creator intensely admired and herself practised. Perhaps more
forcibly than any other character (for all protest too much),
Linton's violation of commonplace assumptions about gender,
and of the conventional ethos of Thrushcross Grange itself,
expresses those qualities of will which the Promethean mentality
most cherishes. In this recreation of human character by a radical
novelist, the existing social code is contradicted or adapted at will.

The genuine affection and regard which exist between
Catherine and Linton—and which are mutually felt, if perversely
expressed by Catherine—earn him the place on one side of his wife
which he occupies at the end of the novel, and which Heathcliff

cannot wish, or dig, or spirit away. There is a sense in which she belongs with him and would be incomplete without him, just as if she cut herself off from the daylight conscious self and entered into contractual union exclusively with the dream-world. The novel insists that we need to be related both to our double and to our opposite. 'Lintons', more easily than 'Earnshaws', are capable of a natural process of growing up, casting off outgrown habits of mind without regret. They read, as Edgar does in his study, and as Catherine, Heathcliff and Hareton refuse to do, as a way of not registering or adapting to outside realities through the mediation of books. To refuse to read means a willed stopping at boundaries, and a refusal to 'read' our own world, understanding the characters amongst which we place our signatures. As readers of *Wuthering Heights* we are perusing a book which is about reading and its relation to reality. Through our reading of the novel we are able to come to a limited understanding of the events, as incomplete as the interpretation we can make of the world about us, but as absolutely necessary. It is both like looking into a mirror, and through a window. The first Catherine, the non-reader, and the second, the reader, exemplify both these kinds of perception. Catherine, interned in her bedroom (the capsule of self) entertaining herself by concentration on her own tumultuously interesting ego, is beside herself with rage to imagine that Edgar has been sitting in his room quietly reading a book. It is this glimpsed possibility that Edgar could be less than absorbed in her, communing with other minds, that brings a first, belated and painful moral recognition to Catherine, as if the adult world caught her unawares:

> "But I begin to fancy you don't like me. How strange! I thought, though everyone hated and despised each other, they could not avoid loving me—they have all turned to enemies in a few hours."

From being the heroine of her own story, automatically the subject of every sentence, the hurtful fact dawns that amongst the many woven stories in the world, hers only counts for one. Reading the expressions around her, she is able to put forth a small, quickened shoot of moral awareness, very late.

Paradoxically, Edgar the book-lover is really only interested in Catherine's story and the art of reading her. In the passage which relates his more than motherly care during her convalescence, his nature tries to speak to hers in its own language. His bringing of the first March crocuses to lay upon her pillow reminds her of the first thaws at the Heights, where the crocus is the first of the new spring flowers:

> "Catherine, last spring, at this time, I was longing to have you under this roof—now, I wish you were a mile or two up those hills: the air blows so sweetly, I feel that it would cure you."
>
> "I shall never be there, but once more!" said the invalid; "and then you'll leave me, and I shall remain, for ever. Next spring you'll long again to have me under this roof, and you'll look back and think you were happy to-day."

In this dialogue there is an emphasis on the cyclical rhythms of nature in a three-fold process, as last spring turns to this spring and round again to the next, while the speakers' moods sway from memory to prophecy and then prophecy of new memory. Catherine is lachrymose in her illness, playing feebly with Edgar's emotions, needing to be wanted by him, and wanting him to start mourning her now, so that she can have the satisfaction of being here to see it. Edgar moves into the future upon the momentum of a wish—that she could leave his house—which turns back into the past, for he is wishing her back to what she was. Catherine sombrely projects herself into the future: ' "you'll leave me" ', which becomes ' "you'll long" ', and finally doubles back, ' "you'll look back" '. She predicts herself into the past tense, over and done with, like every story. But throughout the novel Linton has been associated with spring, fertility, the cycle of nature; with youth and dawning sunlight. The 'handful of golden crocuses' which he brings is an emblem of this golden and life-giving being, just as their daughter Cathy will be identified with the pale gold of primroses. This association with the delicate yellow flowers whose brief emergence preludes the death of death, makes us think also of Catherine, who is dying, in terms of a rebirth which soothes the fretful riddle of tenses: what has been, will be, will have been. She needs Linton, for he bears 'soft thaw winds, and warm sunshine, and nearly melted snow', the secret of a ripening future. Even in her abuse of him, therefore, a clinging need or a claim is felt. At the onset of her illness she had said:

"You are one of those things that are ever found when least
wanted, and when you are wanted, never! I suppose we shall
have plenty of lamentations now . . . I see we shall . . . but
they can't keep me from my narrow home out yonder—my
resting-place where I'm bound before Spring is over! There it
is, not among the Lintons, mind, under the chapel-roof, but
in the open air with a head-stone; and you may please
yourself, whether you go to them, or come to me!"

Linton is demoted from a person to a 'thing'. It is the child's
furious withdrawal of trust (' "you may please yourself" ') in
return for imagined neglect. Though Catherine goes on to say ' "I
don't want you, Edgar; I'm past wanting you" ', the form in
which she discounts him covertly admits to having wanted him in
the past and predicts his vulnerability, in retribution for having
cared for his precious books rather than her precious self. It is not
a case of a conventionally adulterous preference extinguishing a
married love: Emily Brontë's heroine is held in continuous tension
between the twin poles of her nature. There is no slackening of this
pull of oppositions, nor can they be reconciled in her life-time. The
eternal binding and stretching of the three entities—Linton,
Catherine, Heathcliff—is symbolized by Linton's lying asleep
beside her corpse on her death-bed, with Heathcliff lingering
adjacent in the park outside; by Nelly's weaving of the strands of
the hair of the three together in the locket which will rest on
Catherine's heart in her grave; finally by the three parallel
headstones on the slope of the graveyard with the moor creeping
up to reclaim and unify them.

    Perhaps more fully and precisely than anywhere else in
Wuthering Heights, the mystery of the triple bond which links not
only Heathcliff and Linton alternately to the central figure of
Catherine but also most deeply to one another, is to be found in
Catherine's declaration containing the justly famous phrase 'I *am*
Heathcliff', which most readers sense as presenting a shadowy
clue to the novel. Catherine here is only seventeen, wears her heart
on her sleeve, says whatever comes into her head. In the midst of
an adolescent muddle of emotions is set one of the most moving
and least explicable prose-poems in our language. The episode is
defined by Nelly as a 'catechism', and though this is intended
mockingly Catherine is genuinely drawn into the assertion of a

creed concerning her most essential faiths and values. Nelly gets her to admit that, seen in a certain light, her fancy for Linton may appear superficial. Her ' "I love the ground under his feet, and the air over his head" ' is childish parody of the stock attitudes of romantic love. Catherine likes his good looks and is attracted by his property. When it is put to her that in taking Linton she must shed Heathcliff, she interrupts indignantly:

> "Have you considered how you'll bear the separation, and how he'll bear to be quite deserted in the world? Because, Miss Catherine—"
> "He quite deserted! we separated!" she exclaimed, with an accent of indignation. "Who is to separate us, pray? They'll meet the fate of Milo! Not as long as I live, Ellen—for no mortal creature. Every Linton on the face of the earth might melt into nothing, before I could consent to forsake Heathcliff. Oh, that's not what I intend—that's not what I mean!"

Emily Brontë is writing in an ancient tradition of English poetry and drama, adapted to the novel form, embedding in the ground of her story deeply-rooted but inconspicuous emblems and allusions to myth or literature. Lockwood dropped a chance reference to Shakespeare's *King Lear* when he had first visited Wuthering Heights, so that it seemed for a moment that the moors of Emily Brontë's novel could be mapped so as to shade in to the heath of Shakespeare's play, with its pain of loss and exposure, its unbearable questions about human nature, and the strange laughter of the fool (here Joseph) lighting a path. Here, the reference to the myth of Milo casts a sudden brilliant light on Catherine's predicament, and the life-structures the novel is exploring. Milo, the unconquerable Greek athlete, sought to demonstrate his skill by splitting the trunk of a living tree with his bare hands; the tree closed on his hands, and he was eaten by wolves. The tree suggests a mysterious power of nature, not actively hostile to humanity but murderously aroused by ill-judged interference to prevent violation. Heathcliff and Catherine together in their kinship are, in this application of the legend, also kin to the magic tree: Linton would stand in the role of Milo, offering himself like a lamb to the slaughter.

The tree embodies Heathcliff and Catherine, not as 'twins' but as sharers of one being. A tree's deep roots suggest a timeless and enduring permanency; the Tree of Life; the tree of genealogy. The 'Linton' attribute of Catherine is revealed by contrast as an adopted social role rather than an essential part of her nature: though she will be 'Mrs' Linton, the change of status will not, she is sure, make her any the less 'Catherine', an imperishable individual whose nature is one with Heathcliff's, rooted in the greater nature which is their inheritance. No Heathcliff, no Catherine. As she sweeps Linton aside in an extravagant rhetorical gesture, along with all his family, saying that 'every Linton on the face of the earth might melt into nothing', his facial beauty suggests that he belongs only on the surface of her mind, its face. Yet as she develops the theme, she subtly changes the formulation to show the implicit bond linking her two suitors, for 'if I marry Linton, I can aid Heathcliff'. Though this is meant only to refer to money-matters, and displays a wonderful ignorance of the likely reaction of her intended to having his wealth channelled into a rival's pockets, it is also introducing a new emphasis to the emotional logic: 'if Linton, then Heathcliff'. Linton is to be used to raise Heathcliff from his raw and buried condition of propertylessness. If everybody involved will co-operate, it seems to Catherine a very workable plan.

But it is Catherine herself who corresponds with 'Milo' seeking to split the tree; she who will be devoured by wolves. Her vain-glorious ' "Who is to separate us, pray?" ' is answered by Heathcliff at the centre of the novel, ' "*you*, of your own will, did it" ', and recognized in her penitent ' "I'm dying for it" '. When Catherine chooses to go in, to Thrushcross Grange, and down, to the valley, the vagrant part of her remains incapable of restraint in the 'outside' world. Going in to Linton's gentler, harmonious and oil-lit world, she cannot pull the 'dark' self in with her. Catherine becomes Milo, thinking herself the incomparable athlete who can separate herself out and not be split; imagining that she can force the oppositions within her nature to play into one another's hands. These oppositions are shown as incapable of coercion; the power to be reconciled comes from the tree of life itself, heredity in the second generation achieving by natural magic what will-power in the first could not. Yet the second generation is tamer, less alive to us as readers, not because of any lessening of narrative power but by the very nature of their condition. The strange aura and power of the subconscious world shines through the first Catherine's capricious and unlikable personality with an incomparable beauty, like buried mineral wealth dimly glowing, captured in rhythms, images, and stresses which her daughter can never reach. The first Catherine, through being so out of control, is a dreamer, a poet. The greatest speeches in the novel are mainly hers. The paradox of the unconscious world is that, if it is brought to light in a reasonable way, it will seldom bear looking at. The images which in our dreams shocked us with beauty and meaning are found upon inspection inert and disappointing, out of their fluent element. Emily Brontë appears to have accepted the Romantic idea that the poet (as dreamer or mystic) is in some sense crippled or incapacitated for everyday life by those very gifts or insights which are so prodigally bestowed on her or him. While her poems speak of not wanting to live other than nocturnally, her life history tells of not being able to. 'The Philosopher's Conclusion' explains this reluctance in terms of a myth of triple self-division:

> "I saw a Spirit standing, Man,
> Where thou dost stand—an hour ago;
> And round his feet, three rivers ran
> Of equal depth and equal flow—
>
> "A Golden stream, and one like blood,
> And one like Sapphire, seemed to be,
> But where they joined their triple flood
> It tumbled in an inky sea.
>
> "The Spirit bent his dazzling gaze
> Down on that Ocean's gloomy night,
> Then—kindling all with sudden blaze,
> The glad deep sparkled wide and bright—
> White as the sun; far, far more fair
> Than the divided sources were!"

The 'divided sources' of the self, each stained a brilliant cardinal colour, flow to a mutual outlet in her art. But the 'Spirit' whose eyes can turn the black sea of ink to the unity of white which contains all colours is lost. The idea of a threefold division is unmistakably reminiscent of *Wuthering Heights*. Catherine, whose dreams go through her kindled self, and do not die in the light of

day but are handed to us intact in the unparaphrasable poetry of
her speeches, speaks from self-division, seeks reconciliation but
can only reach it in oblivion. The novel tells the disappointing
truth that the crippling effects of this heightened insight are not
compensated for in this life. The moment of ecstasy and of
utterance has a power matched only by its brevity. Its aftermath is
a fierce nostalgia, like the gasping of consumptive lungs for
oxygen. The visionary speaker in the poem is deflated into the
feeble wish:

> O for the time when in my breast
> Their struggles will be o'er;
> O for the day when I shall rest
> And never suffer more.

So also Catherine's high hopes are brought down to a defeated
wail for ' "my narrow home . . . my resting place" ', in reaction
after the intoxication of those dreams which had so transformed
her mental colouring as to convince her that contradictory needs
might be reconciled by brute force of wishing.

Catherine explains to Nelly that her motive for marrying
Linton is:

> "for the sake of one who comprehends in his person my
> feelings to Edgar and myself. I cannot express it; but surely
> you and every body have a notion that there is, or should be,
> an existence of yours beyond you. What were the use of my
> creation if I were entirely contained here? My great miseries
> in this world have been Heathcliff's miseries, and I watched
> and felt each from the beginning; my great thought in living is
> himself. If all else perished, and *he* remained, I should still
> continue to be; and, if all else remained, and he were
> annihilated, the Universe would turn to a mighty stranger. I
> should not seem a part of it. My love for Linton is like the
> foliage in the woods. Time will change it, I'm well aware, as
> winter changes the trees—my love for Heathcliff resembles
> the eternal rocks beneath—a source of little visible delight,
> but necessary. Nelly, I *am* Heathcliff—he's always, always in
> my mind—not as a pleasure, any more than I am always a
> pleasure to myself—but, as my own being—so, don't talk of
> our separation again—it is impractical; and—"

Catherine's 'always, always' mimes a child's insistence on its fixed idea; she pushes her face into the folds of Nelly's dress like a little girl who, having given a secret away, asks to be indulged and confirmed. But equally her 'always, always' represents the continuity of consciousness itself. This is an adult's speech, rooted in a child's postures, bearing a proud answer to philosophy's eternal questions, 'What and who am I, and who is kin to me?' The first half of the speech is a carefully framed argument, in terms of intellectual abstraction, for the existence in Catherine's life of a mirror to her self, in which her nature is reflected and validated. But the mirror is doubly and reciprocally reflecting, for Heathcliff mirrors himself within her, through her sympathetic identification from earliest childhood with his rejection: ' "I watched and felt . . . from the beginning." ' She does not so much claim to have been born with a predestined 'twin' as explain that the two have grown to contain one another. The growing-together has created the sacred bond. The meditation for all its cosmic applications, is oddly rational and sensible, because of its roots in the experience of the miracle of a child's loneliness salved and shared. In her poem of 1845, 'No coward soul', Emily Brontë set forth the idea of a 'God within my breast', projected on to the natural world as Catherine's soul is projected on to Heathcliff:

> Though Earth and moon were gone
> And suns and universes ceased to be
> And thou wert left alone
> Every Existence would exist in thee

In Catherine's statement of identity with Heathcliff, such blissful confidence as the poem expresses is undercut by the poignant awareness that it might be all too possible to survive the death of one's 'twin', and to be left alien upon a foreign landscape. Her faith is not safely bestowed within the narcissistically hoarding self but upon a fellow mortal whom it might be possible to imagine as 'annihilated'. In her speech, persons and places are almost indistinguishable. Heathcliff is a place to be; the universe is a person, who might turn into a 'stranger', that most threatening word in Emily Brontë's vocabulary. The dream-quality of the speech has an underlying edge of nightmare, which surfaces as the possibility of separation becomes more real to the speaker and her serenely commanding grasp of an argument begins to falter and break down. The elegance of immaculately grammatical sentences is disrupted into breathless phrases strung on a punctuation composed solely of dashes.

The grandiose faith declared in 'No coward soul' is challenged by no contradictory loyalty or desire, such as the 'Linton' element of the self which exerts over Catherine the positive power of all gentle and lovable beings. The acknowledgement of his power is made in terms of the imagery of nature and the seasonal cycle as Catherine struggles to define the character of her affection for him so that Nelly will be able to understand how different this is from her kinship with Heathcliff, and how compatible with it: 'like the foliage in the woods', as against Heathcliff's 'eternal rocks beneath'. The movement of her mind to Linton is upward to a place above the surface, coming out of burial into psychologically clement air and light, 'on the face of the earth'. In associating her love for him with the foliage of trees, she declares an affinity with all that is changeful and beautiful in the natural world, flower, bird, leaf, shedding themselves only to recur. Heathcliff neither loves nor cherishes this kind of life. When Catherine tells Isabella of his nature, she draws imagery from the harsh, underlying landscape in its predatory relationship to the vulnerable creatures of the upper world:

> "Tell her what Heathcliff is—an unreclaimed creature, without refinement—without cultivation; an arid wilderness of furze and whinstone. I'd as soon put that little canary into the park on a winter's day as recommend you to bestow your heart on him! ... He's not a rough diamond—a pearl-containing oyster of a rustic; he's a fierce, pitiless, wolfish man. ... he'd crush you like a sparrow's egg, Isabella ... There's my picture; and I'm his friend. ..."

Heathcliff's personality, described as 'unreclaimed' has its own sort of raw beauty which even in this polemic based on his ugly attributes is registered in the very mention of the emotive 'wilderness of furze and whinstone'. You long to wander there even while recognizing the destructiveness of a 'wolfish' nature which eats alive Linton lambs like Isabella. In the manner of a sadistic child it would stamp down the frail-shelled sparrow's egg; it is fruitless like winter to the warm blood of the delicate indoor canary, 'arid' and sterile. There is a deep need for more than this bedrock of unreclaimed human nature: a balancing need for the fruitful beauty of a love that is 'like the foliage in the woods', natural, rhythmic, self-renewing. The movement toward Linton represents entrance into the cyclical pattern of change and rebirth.

More deeply still, the two images, seeming so opposite, are one. The darkness of the subconscious and the light of the conscious self belong to the same mind: the rocks beneath are a basis for the cyclical life which proceeds in the upper world. The mediating image is that of a tree, whose unity in the legend of Milo could not be split, and which sinks its roots deep into the lower world to spread boughs and leaves into the upper one. In this implied image, the transience and variety of vegetation are reconciled with the permanence of roots which grip the earth. Linton and Heathcliff complete one another, as the two halves of a single mind, or as 'female' and 'male', time and eternity. The image of Catherine's love for Linton as 'the foliage in the woods' looks forward through the novel's sequences of echoes and reflections to Heathcliff standing rooted to the spot by the ash tree at the Grange during the birth of Cathy and the death of her mother, and to the new generation in which Cathy would grow 'like a larch'.

In *Wuthering Heights*, it is as if we are born with both an identical and a fraternal twin, so that the condition of fruitful existence depends on making a viable relationship with each. In the first generation (the 'old testament') such rooting could only take place when personality, with its bias, agitations and split loyalties, has been shed, and the individualities of Catherine, Linton and Heathcliff have perished into the moor. Room has been made for the second generation, in a new testament, to effect their own reconciliation in this life. For the first, reconciliation lies in the moorland itself, a source and an end, refusing no one admittance, knowing no preferences and entertaining no hostility. The novel has, fittingly, a double ending, presenting opposite conclusions of its story, neither of them authoritative. On the one hand we may believe with the superstitious local people that the ghosts of Catherine and Heathcliff walk the moors together. Nelly records meeting a terrified small boy with some sheep and lambs:

"They's Heathcliff and a woman, yonder, under t'Nab," he blubbered, "un' Aw darnut pass 'em."
I saw nothing; but neither the sheep nor he would go on . . .

The behaviour of the boy is easy to explain away, as Nelly uneasily tries to by reference to the ghostly stories rife in the community; the instinctive behaviour of the sheep possibly less so. The author leaves it open, passing swiftly to the other narrator who, as he began the telling, will end it, and now offers the second and opposite solution—that the dead sleep soundly, and together. The only evidence for this lies in the look of the three graves side by side at the edge of the decaying churchyard:

> I sought, and soon discovered, the three head-stones on the slope next the moor—the middle one grey, and half buried in heath—Edgar Linton's only harmonised by the turf, and moss creeping up its foot—Heathcliff's still bare.

Each grave is involved in a different stage in the process of reversion to the moor, which is also claiming the derelict church. When the process is complete, each grave will be equally and wholly covered over with heath. The deletion of individual identity is felt as positive and recreative; its effect is one of formal and mathematical symmetry, with the extremes of Catherine's nature one on either side. The green of grass and moss on Edgar's headstone evokes the 'beautiful fertile valley' with which he had been associated; Heathcliff's 'bare' stone calls to mind the 'eternal rocks' with which his identification has been. Each quietly flanks and frames the central stone. The central stone itself is dual, for it is 'half' buried in heath. At the very ending, we are aware of a state of transition, a process not yet complete. The grave of each person is at a certain point in its continuing process toward reconciliation. At the point where the moors have reclaimed the graves entirely, and rubbed out the writing on the headstones so that human identity is deleted, the code which has characterized this novel will be finally broken. To the avidly unsatisfied reader, names have been problems throughout the novel. Strange alliterations and vowel-music allowed us to guess at an underlying pattern or harmony—Hareton, Heathcliff, Hindley—but it was never possible to spell the intuited pattern out. The novel, like writing itself, and like the texture of experience in the world outside the novel, has been something incompletely legible. We never knew where we were, exactly, sharing Lockwood's predicament riddling at his first visit to the Heights. In the pattern of the three graves, the three names which had so worryingly danced before Lockwood's eyes—Catherine Earnshaw, Catherine Linton, Catherine Heathcliff—have stilled into the one Catherine at rest between her two loves. What the reader is left with is not so much a sense of individual personalities as the living presence of the moor itself, surrounding and gaining upon the human scene in the closing part of the novel, until in Lockwood's final paragraph, sky, heath and grass, 'breathed' over by a soft wind, become—rather than a passive background for the events that have been, and beyond the moor's containment of the three characters folded together within the earth—the ultimate subject of the novel:

> I lingered round them, under that benign sky, watched the moths fluttering among the heath and hare-bells; listened to the soft wind breathing through the grass; and wondered how any one could ever imagine unquiet slumbers for the sleepers in that quiet earth.

9 The Mother Beneath the Earth

A New Testament

It was far in the night, and the bairnies grat,
The mither beneath the mools heard that.

CATHY'S eventual mate, Hareton Earnshaw, is—like her—a
means of return to source. In learning from Cathy how to spell and
write his name, he is also able to assert his identity as the heir of
the founder of Wuthering Heights. The first words which are read
by a character within the novel are his name, 'Hareton
Earnshaw', which Lockwood reads carved over the door of the
house, along with the date, 1500. Hareton is a central figure, who
is born in the first half of the book and belongs with the original
generation, but plays his part in the second with Catherine Linton
and Linton Heathcliff. He is born of a mother whom his birth
helps to kill—pretty, inconsequent Frances, an outsider with
Lintonish characteristics: a premonition of the baby Cathy's
destruction of Catherine. Like Cathy, Hareton is born of a deep
and enduring love. When we reach Nelly's account of Catherine's
dying 'like a lamb', stretching like a child, we may recall the
memory of Frances' final gesture in this life, and the memory is
like a wraith: 'she put her two arms about his (Hindley's) neck,
her face changed, and she was dead'. The two mothers—like
Emily's own—last long enough only to see in the new. It is with
the birth of Hareton that Nelly herself graduates into her full role
as foster-mother to the infancies of these bereaved children:
though she has cared for the elder Catherine and for Heathcliff as
children, and played with Hindley as a boy, this is her first baby,
and the first sentence of Chapter VII celebrates the joy with which
she received Hareton: 'On the morning of a fine June day, my first
bonny nursling, and the last of the ancient Earnshaw stock, was
born.' Hareton's unifying role is clear from his first moment in the
world: he is the first and the last. The time of day, the season and
the weather are all significant. June is the mid-point of the year:
the prognostications for this baby in the morning of his life are
'fine'. This is not immediately apparent since his mother is to be

152

lost so soon, and Hindley's love, embittered and coarsened by the pain of his loss, will be about as fruitful and nurturing as the scissors with which he drunkenly proposes to crop his son's unnecessary ears. Yet it is true that Hareton, conceived as a child of love, is welcomed into a world that is glad to receive him. Nelly's love for this 'bonny little nursling' connects him with her tenderness for Cathy, 'the most winning thing that ever brought sunshine into a desolate house'; identifies them almost as brother and sister. In a way that is both like and unlike Catherine's and Heathcliff's obsessive identification, they too 'are' each other very deeply, beneath the level both of words and of consciousness. But Nelly is not, in the long run, accurate in naming Hareton 'the last of the ancient Earnshaw stock'. In the image of Cathy and Hareton, 'her light shining ringlets blending . . . with his brown locks' toward the end of the novel, we see the projection into the future of the ancient stock, renewed and refreshed by the blood of Frances and Edgar Linton, and likely to bear fruit both hardy and sweet. The Earnshaw blood is not only rinsed by outsiders' blood, but its power is doubled. Both Cathy and Hareton are Earnshaws, the female power raised to equal status with the male. We sense that a new cycle is being initiated, so that, the mythic circle having turned once, fully, through 300 years, is at the point of apparent stasis and will find in completion a new beginning.

The rise of Hareton is the fall of Heathcliff. He is Heathcliff's natural opponent in the novel, and they are linked in an organic way which the author, secretive and exceptionally assured in her willingness to leave questions open, clues retained, does not explain. As Heathcliff is degraded by Hindley in the first half of the novel, not educated, used as a servant and abused as an inferior, so Heathcliff conceiving a loathing for Hareton as the true heir, revenges himself by degrading him in turn. Hareton returns Heathcliff's enmity with an infatuated, loyal and tender love. At the end, Hareton 'dug green sods, and laid them over the brown mound (of Heathcliff's grave) himself', greening the grave with turf, conferring a kind of life upon the carcass of one who had abused him but who was profoundly identified with him. There is a silent sub-plot. It is as still and implicit as the moor itself, underlying all the events in Emily's novel. Heathcliff has, against his inclinations, practised a unique fidelity and kindness in respect to Hareton—as if by predestined instinct. We may first encounter this sub-plot at the point where Hareton as a baby frantically kicking and roaring in his appalling father's arms, is accidentally held over the banister by Hindley, leaps, and falls to a certain death, but that:

> Heathcliff arrived underneath just at the critical moment; by a natural impulse, he arrested his descent, and setting him on his feet, looked up to discover the author of the accident.

This is part of a scene of broad and wicked farce, in which Hindley has invited Nelly to eat a carving-knife which she with superb deadpan 'spat out, and affirmed it tasted detestably'; the baby throughout is bawling at the top of its voice; Heathcliff has missed his chance of repaying Hindley, betrayed by his own reflex actions into saving the baby's life. He stands gaping as if a miser had forfeited 'a lucky lottery ticket' for five shillings only to find it would have won five thousand pounds. The incidental money-metaphor expertly preludes Heathcliff's later successful capitalistic enterprises, his avarice, and the final unwilled collapse of his desire to cash his winnings at Cathy's and Hareton's expense. Hindley stupid with drink looking down at Heathcliff stupid with rage stand mirroring one another in ironic juxtaposition: with hindsight the narrator is amused and so are we. But the joke broadens into a wider suggestion: that there is a kind of fate or bias working through 'accidents' of personality, coincidence of events, toward a creative synthesis. This bias only lets Hareton fall into outstretched arms, the embrace of the enemy who 'must' befriend him. Obscurely, they have common cause. Equally this bias forces Heathcliff to act against his conscious interests: he sets the child on its feet. Later, with only the most malign of intentions, he will lure the second Cathy to the Heights, introduce her to Hareton, prepare the way for their union, against his will. Hareton will love and mourn for him, placing over the grave the turf that will lie like a counterpane above his shared resting-place with Cathy's mother. Each central character will mediate for the other, according to some law of nature which works through and for them all. Catherine, she has said, *is* Heathcliff. It would be possible to go further than this and to say that beyond this single identification all the characters are interchangeable. Hareton is Heathcliff is Hindley: the hieroglyphs of their strange, chiming names link them in a chain of a larger destiny, beyond the messages inscribed on their genes or their encounters with conditioning. Tracing them all back to childhood and seeing it still indelible on their adult character, we sense a throng of wraith-like children which gathers through the book: our dead selves, our dead. They are identical, and identically forgiven. In the course of *Wuthering Heights,* they either come to lie together under the earth, or to inhabit the world of fertile union above it. Whether the dead lie quiet or haunt is not said, but left open. The dead can no longer, it is suggested, substantially harm the living.

In this reading of *Wuthering Heights,* Emily Brontë's loss of her mother at the age of 3 has been the single most salient biographical fact. Mother and child in the novel as in life are separated. The mother-principle is under the earth. Yet it does not sleep and has not been neutralized. It speaks through Nelly as narrator, and lives through her as the guardian and foster-mother of the people in the novel (including Lockwood, the apparently 'outer' narrator, whom she nurses in his illness). It structures the events from beyond the grave, enclosing all that transpires. Nelly voices the theme in the scene in which Heathcliff breaks Hareton's fall. She replies angrily to Hindley:

> "Injured! . . . If he's not killed, he'll be an idiot! Oh! I wonder his mother does not rise from her grave to see how you use him. You're worse than a heathen—treating your own flesh and blood in that manner!"

Reflecting on the way that Hareton's future safety has just been ensured, we may consider that the metaphorical equivalent of maternal intervention has just taken place. Nelly's denunciation of Hindley is so round and flavoured with Yorkshire inflection as to forbid—with the supernatural tact of the author's narrative irony—any deduction that this is the 'real' meaning of the passage. Her outburst of vituperation comes of protective fear for the little boy, mingled with cathartic relief at his safety: she falls back on superstition, awakened ghosts, violated taboos. Yet the passage has an eery resonance, given the fact that we have (through Lockwood's dream) already seen into the frame of a world in which the ghosts of dead children haunt and call, and in which Lockwood is given the impression by Heathcliff that there may be something 'out there', which is only dormant, not asleep.

We would be ready to give some credence to the notion that Hareton's mother's spirit might wake for him. Nelly reinforces this image when she goes on to open the conversation with Catherine in which the young girl declares her love for Linton and (after the eavesdropping Heathcliff has crept away) her absolute identification with Heathcliff:

> I was rocking Hareton on my knee, and humming a song that began;
> "It was far in the night, and the bairnies grat,
> The mither beneath the mools heard that,"
> when Miss Cathy . . . put her head in . . .

The lullaby Nelly is singing might be calculated to make the baby's hair stand on end, for it is from 'The Ghaist's Warning', an old Scandinavian ballad which Emily Brontë had found in a volume of Scott's poetry. The father of a family of seven children remarries after their mother's death, and the step-mother harshly rejects them:

> Nor ale nor mead to the bairnies she gave:
> "But hunger and hate frae me ye's have.
>
> She took frae them the bowster blae,
> And said, "Ye sall ligg i' the bare strae!"
>
> She took frae them the groff wax-light:
> Says, "Now ye sall ligg i' the mirk a' night!"
>
> 'Twas lang i' the night, and the bairnies grat:
> Their mither she under the mools heard that.

The mother, hearing her little ones crying from 'under the mools' (the earth), petitions the Lord for permission to return and put them to rights. At first she appals and terrifies them, for she returns as she is, an animated corpse; then she combs, dresses and plays with them, even going so far as to suckle the hungry baby from her dead breast. Finally she rebukes her husband for his neglect and threatens him with evil fortune if she ever has occasion to reappear. In one of the most poignant details, one of the elder children offers to stand in place of the true mother toward the others:

> Up spak little Kirstin in bed that lay:
> "To thy bairnies I'll do the best I may."

The ballad is in equal measure spine-chilling and heart-breaking. Its homely details are charged with an atmosphere of primitive horror as the world of the dead intersects with the world of the living. Yet the ghost is less dreadful than the step-mother's malignant cruelty; the unknown darkness of the other world appears less hostile than that of the one in which we live, personified in the step-mother's utterly believable words of gall to the unwanted infants. Withdrawing their food, warmth, light and shelter, she evokes in them a grief that cries out so poignantly, so loudly and so late into the night that it has power to wake the dead. In quoting from the ballad, Emily Brontë reinforces her theme of bereaved and rejected children, including the plight of Hareton. As 'little Kirstin' moves over to fill the place of the lost mother (as Maria, then Charlotte, had done in Emily's life), so Nelly takes over the unwanted children who pass through her capable and mainly willing hands. In a larger sense, the ballad speaks of a capacity in the world beyond this one both to terrorize and (simultaneously) benignly to restructure this one. It tells of natural love as enduring not only beyond but within the grave. The unkindnesses suffered above ground may be mitigated in extreme need by the fearful irruption of the dead, clad in the decaying remnants of their mortal bodies, over the boundaries of mortality. There is a principle of goodness and natural solicitude at the heart of all that is most feared. *Wuthering Heights* testifies that love survives.

This deep and close relationship postulated between the dead and the living—not just their spirits but their bodies too—reaches into the heart of Emily Brontë's novel. Nelly conventionally sees Catherine's spirit as forsaking the empty shell of her body for some other world beyond the carnate. Heathcliff digs deeper. Eighteen years after her death he gets the sexton to open up her grave and looks at her face. Nelly is not only horrified at the impiety of this but aware of the grisly practicalities involved:

"And if she had been dissolved into earth, or worse, what would you have dreamt of then?" I said.

"Of dissolving with her, and being more happy still!" he answered. "Do you suppose that I dread any change of that sort? I expected such a transformation on raising the lid, but I'm better pleased that it should not commence till I share it."

Emily Brontë may well be interested in making her reader shiver with that common and lurid enjoyment of horror with which the Gothic novel and the horror-film experiment. But more profoundly she probes beyond the limits of moral and social categories into an extended perspective, both backwards to source and forward to our destination. Her novel tries to 'see' as if through some newly invented optical instrument where we came from (what existed before our beginning?) and where we shall go (what comes after the end?). It sees this in material terms, not just abstractions. Like Heathcliff cracking off the screws on the coffin, we are asked to look into the darkness at the future self when individuality shall have perished, and being is immobile, insentient, blind and unseen. It is upon this dreadful candour of vision that Emily Brontë erects a faith. She takes the reader to look down into a tomb at a palpable death, and then denies its elimination of character. The corruption of Catherine's corpse, returning to something 'worse' than earth—the putrescence which Nelly will not mention exactly and does not want to think about—is ruefully admitted in this vision as inevitable; then it is affirmed as positive and valuable. The frightening noun 'dissolution' becomes in both Nelly's and Heathcliff's usage the strangely consolatory verb 'to dissolve', suggesting a fluid reconciliation with the being of another person. If it is seen in this way, then how—as Heathcliff asks in irritation—could one 'dread any change of that sort?' He perceives decay not as annihilation or destruction but as a positive 'transformation', a reshaping into some form more natural and new.

Heathcliff is aware of the living presence of Catherine as a moving spirit on the earth: she lies in wait for him just out of range of, his eyesight. No author has more accurately expressed the quality of paradox in a nearly, but not quite, assuaged desire: ' "My soul's bliss kills my body, but does not satisfy itself." ' This feeling of being 'killed with desire' is very like the sensation described in Emily's visionary poems. Heathcliff's half-a-lifetime of reaching after an apparition which mocks him with the certainty of its presence even when it eludes him, arouses a terminal joy. The author of *Wuthering Heights* carefully allows us to feel that this persistent haunting by Catherine, so that Heathcliff cannot close his eyes at night without opening them just to make sure he cannot see her, may be viewed, if we prefer, as a function of

his own obsessed, insomniac psychology. Variation in readers'
temperament and credulity is consistently allowed for, while the
novel stretches a highly-wrought tension between the subjective
and the objective interpretations. These are prudent tactics with
such sensational materials, so that by an art of self-defence
habitually practised in her daily life, the author herself never
appears, but lets Lockwood say that Nelly reported that
Heathcliff had related his haunting. The picture at this moment is
enclosed within three separate frames. Nevertheless, there is a
powerful sense that what we see reflected at three removes is a core
image which is all the more simply real because it is not affirmed.
Heathcliff's bare, eloquent account asserts a meaning which we
accept both as true for him and, if not rationally explicable, true in
some sense for us too:

> "And when I slept in her chamber—I was beaten out of
> that—I couldn't lie there; for the moment I closed my eyes,
> she was either outside the window, or sliding back the panels,
> or entering the room, or even resting her darling head on the
> same pillow as she did when a child."

All his images are of Catherine coming in: in to the house, in to the
bed, in to the room, in to his arms. In fact, she only comes in to his
mind. But Catherine cursed him, in our hearing, with the promise
of haunting him, and there is no ridding oneself of the sensation
that she might just in some 'real' way be there, in person, as
Heathcliff suspects, capricious and childishly mocking to her
dying day and beyond. The panelled bed is an image of place
which is alive with associations accrued for us throughout the
novel. Lockwood's nightmare waif sought him there; the panel of
the coffin which the sexton has just been bribed to slide away
mirrors the panel of the bed; Catherine had imagined herself back
there in her last illness 'laid alone, for the first time', with the fresh
pain of separation which is the same for every character and never
grows old. Catherine's ' "I was a child' " is a refrain caught up
here in Heathcliff's 'as she did when a child'. In being subject to
these repeated echoes and rhythms as we read, we—like
Lockwood—are drawn in, below the level of consciousness
perhaps, to participate in the experiences of the characters.
Heathcliff's grief is that what he so vividly recalls he cannot
actually call up. The feeling that he might be able to is equivalent

to physical assault: ' "I was beaten out of that." ' Emily Brontë
defines mental events as if they were physical and could 'beat' at
you, so that the pilgrimage through life from source (the panelled
bed) to end (the panelled coffin) requires nerves of 'catgut' to
make it endurable.

Heathcliff's cruelty shocked the sensibilities of the first
generation of the novel's readers. This cruelty is echoed in each of
the trio of characters whose names begin with 'H', from Hindley's
brutality to the usurping foster-son, to Hareton's incidental
'hanging a litter of puppies from a chair-back in the doorway'. It is
present too in Catherine's wicked tongue; in Joseph's grotesque
conception of divine hate; in a weakened form in Linton
Heathcliff, that 'sickly slip' of humanity; and perhaps in Isabella
Linton, though we have only Heathcliff's word for it that ' "no
brutality disgusted her" '. Yet each squalid adult is also shown as
a piteous victim, at the mercy of genetic inheritance and
conditioning. The scheme of justice affirmed is like that not very
workable sort which is evolved by Shakespeare's King Lear:
'None does offend, none, I say none', and with this sturdy
abstention from casting blame Emily Brontë vigorously blocks
access to any moral resting-place dependent on a chosen
scapegoat. We come to feel that Hindley, in forcibly separating
Catherine and Heathcliff from one another's company, might be
suitable for this role, but it is Nelly who, departing from her
function of disinterested observer, messenger and care-taker,
disappoints us. On Hindley's behalf, Nelly enters the dream-
world which she more usually frames and communicates. She, like
Lockwood, is, it seems, capable of a more than daylight vision.
About ten months after she has lost care of Hareton, on her way to
the village, she reaches the sign-post on the cross-roads, where
the initials for Gimmerton, Wuthering Heights and Thrushcross
are cut upon a stone:

> The sun shone yellow on its grey head, reminding me of
> summer; and I cannot say why, but all at once, a gush of
> child's sensations flowed into my heart. Hindley and I held it
> a favourite spot twenty years before.
>
> I gazed long at the weather-worn block; and, stooping
> down, perceived a hole near the bottom still full of snail-
> shells and pebbles which we were fond of storing there with

more perishable things—and, as fresh as reality, it appeared that I beheld my early playmate seated on the withered turf, his dark, square head bent forward, and his little hand scooping out the earth with a piece of slate.

"Poor Hindley!" I exclaimed, involuntarily.

In ancient traditions, a cross-roads symbolizes death. Here it suggests the intersection of past with present, everyday reality with dream-reality. Even for the prosaic Nelly, being at the cross-roads where the paths to the alternative human communities meet, there is a gap which may open out into the past. It is not found by looking but is come upon by chance, signalled by some apparent change of colour or dimension in the outside world. It is a visionary moment. Just as Catherine's dreams go through her 'like wine through water', with an indelible staining of the fluid of personality by a chemical reaction, as a colourless solution absorbs a red dye, a bright taste, so the grey whinstone of the post takes on a yellow colour from the sunlight, which draws Nelly's eyes. Her eyesight now begins to alter. Where there was winter, she transposes summer; for a dead stone like that which marks a grave, she sees a more living image (there is the 'head' of the stone, the head of the boy); in place of the present she sees the past. Paradoxically the hard stone block induces a mental event which is like a melting of the mind, as though some petrification of past events gave way. Nelly experiences a 'gush' of child's 'sensations' (not thoughts) which 'flowed' into her 'heart' (not mind). Nelly for that special moment obtains access to her old self which is so young, vital, fluid and immediate; she becomes a child again, entering the throng of child selves who cluster in the recesses of the novel. It is involuntary, like dreaming. As Catherine is to Heathcliff, and Cathy will be to Hareton, so, it appears, Nelly is to Hindley, providing a muted echo of the twin theme.

As Nelly moves closer, she sees deeper. At the base of the stone is a little scooped-out hole containing a precious treasure-hoard of 'snail-shells and pebbles': they have been there for twenty years, along with other small items in the children's collection which have passed away, being 'perishable'. Nobody has disturbed this collection, for nobody would think it significant or valuable. But just as the earth will keep the beloved body of Catherine intact, harbouring her until her twin can join her, so the earth conserves in this open receptacle something that is precious for Nelly. These are not dead relics, the aftermath of an outlived phase, but full of power and life—though with the poignancy of things abandoned, like the skeletons of the lapwing chicks in their nest—for they can call up to Nelly's mind the vision of Hindley as a child, 'fresh as reality'. Nelly can see him in detail, and we read her description with a slight sense of shock, for Hindley the child seems to rise to life through the matrix of Nelly's recounting memory, as if we could see his face, slightly from the side and at a short distance (his 'dark, square head'), sitting on the withered turf that speaks of winter and the decay of childhood, and going about his business of harmless, absorbed digging. The endearing 'little hand' scrapes away so realistically with the makeshift 'piece of slate'; Nelly's love for that little hand, and her past participation in the game, deeply touch us. She fears, superstitiously, that this might be a portent of Hindley's death, so supernaturally real does the vision seem: the subtler truth is that the child-Hindley is dead. The fallen adult self has parted company with its original. Nelly's sense of bereavement is entirely justified.

The conclusion Nelly draws from her vision which, being involuntary, is to be trusted, is the simple statement, ' "Poor Hindley" '. Seen from this perspective Hindley receives his exactly equal share of the author's inflexibly measured compassion, upon which each character has unlimited claim. Nelly's vision is composed of those hard elements which stand the test of time—a stone post, a handful of shells and pebbles, a piece of slate. These are objects which we can retain and count on from the past, which will seem nearly imperishable. These hoardings in the earth have no obvious beauty, as there is in the seasonal change of vegetation—trees, grasses, heather. The fragments which compose Nelly's vision are related to 'the eternal rocks beneath' to which Heathcliff is allied. He too is made of 'whinstone'; in his name is the 'cliff' which bears the heath. In Nelly's memory Hindley is seen as 'dark' (Heathcliff's colouring), bending to the earth and holding a fragment of slate, whose colour would be dark-grey. The memory is void of bright colour, lyricism or obvious joy. All children have made such treasure-hoards of objects whose only value lies in the fact that they are our gatherings, touched and named by us. In the light of experience, such hoards represent the frail human hold on his tenancy of the world, and the small winnings each keeps. This universality is germane to the experience of the novel: it is important that we sympathize with Hindley, the remembered child, so that he may be judged only with a gentle eye, for he has no winnings. Heathcliff gets him to gamble and mortgage away his property in his favour. When the author tells of Heathcliff's growing avarice as a 'besetting sin', she indicates that Heathcliff too is doing the adult equivalent of scooping out a place in which to put his valuables. Heathcliff also emerges with no winnings, in material terms, the inheritance reverting to Hareton. Value in *Wuthering Heights* is always and only personal, never material. The treasure held in store for Heathcliff in the earth is the being of Catherine; in his mind, the memory of Catherine. Hindley's scooped-out hollow is also a symbol for human memory itself, the faculty which for Emily Brontë was primary and recreative. Ellen as the tale-teller is the main rememberer in *Wuthering Heights*. The art of narrative is shown to be based on the art of memory, in which the practical and business-like narrator never gets bogged down, save on this one occasion when she is drawn involuntarily into its mesmerizing world. The problem is presented as to how to use the vital resource of memory within the continuum of the present, and project it into the future in such a way as to make survival practicable and desirable. It is put in a very balanced way since the novel recognizes, as does her Gondal poetry, the necessity of leaving the past behind, in some measure closing the mental eyes upon it. This is not despite but because of its beauty and allure. In 'Cold in the earth', Rosina speaks of her fifteen years of bereavement as a process of learning how to extricate herself from her memory:

> Then did I learn how existence could be cherished,
> Strengthened and fed without the aid of joy.

She speaks of the process of letting go as a kind of 'weaning'. The faithful spirit submits to leave the suckling comfort of living in the past, accepting the 'Memory's rapturous pain' is enjoyed at the expense of maturity and independence. In *Wuthering Heights*, Heathcliff feeds on memory and starves himself to death, so preferring the 'rapturous pain' as to be unable to commit himself to any future at all. He is suicidally caught in Catherine's need for him not to forget:

"Will you forget me—will you be happy when I am in the earth? Will you say twenty years hence, 'That's the grave of Catherine Earnshaw. I loved her long ago, and was wretched to lose her; but it is past. I've loved many others since—my children are dearer to me than she was, and, at death, I shall not rejoice that I am going to her, I shall be sorry that I must leave them!' Will you say so, Heathcliff?"

This is the piteous grief of the dying, picturing and realistically pre-enacting a future in which they must in the course of things be superseded, figuring only as a blurred or debased memory. Catherine recognizes that the health of the survivor depends on a suspension of grief that can only be brought about by the ability to say, 'it is past'. Her picture of Heathcliff as the complacent husband and father is ludicrously inappropriate, yet it represents the prescription which common sense and the necessity for the world to go on must offer: the platitude that all grief must ebb, new currents flow. In Catherine's prediction we are allowed to see the parasitical relation between the dying and the living. Emily Brontë at once shows the art of memory as the most creative human resource, and simultaneously and phlegmatically criticizes this perception by insisting on the unlimited destructive powers latent in that resource.

The final development in Nelly's act of memory involves a twist back to the present. What she sees appears to turn in response and to see her reciprocally:

"Poor Hindley!" I exclaimed, involuntarily.
I started—my bodily eye was cheated into a momentary belief that the child lifted its face and stared straight into mine! It vanished in a twinkling; but, immediately, I felt an irresistible yearning to be at the Heights. Superstition urged me to comply with this impulse—supposing he should be dead! I thought—or should die soon!—supposing it were a sign of death!

Immediately after her exclamation the spell begins to break. Nelly the sensible narrator parts company with Nelly the superstitious Yorkshirewoman by commenting on, criticizing and rationalizing what she saw. She now clearly labels herself as 'cheated' into hallucinating, stressing the transience of the impression of the child's—or elf's, or demon's—appearance. The subsequent churning rhythms convey both the storming of her pulse as she makes for the Heights and mime in sarcasm the farce of her superstitious feelings. At the exact point at which the figment of Nelly's imagination threatens to take on autonomous life, Emily Brontë goes to some lengths to undermine the credibility of her impressions. The elf-world which lies at the background of the novel is the recurrent subject of allusion but never of affirmation, restrained from rising up to threaten the coherence of the illusion. Tactfully, the author leaves us guessing as to whether the child's response is just an idle quirk of fancy or whether momentary communication has taken place between two worlds. There is plenty of room for either, or even for both, interpretations.

Nelly has grown up in a world where populations of elves, fairies and mischievous spirits of nature survive in a living folk-lore. She is unsure whether Heathcliff might not be a vampire or ghoul; Catherine calls her a witch; the younger Cathy at the beginning of the novel pretends to be one, to upset Joseph, whose superstitious Christianity is rooted in the primitive conviction that the legions of Satan, probably in female form, are all around him requiring frequent and noisy denunciation:

> "Stop, look here, Joseph . . . I'll show you how far I've progressed in the Black Art—I shall soon be competent to make a clear house of it. The red cow didn't die by chance; and your rheumatism can hardly be reckoned among providential visitations!"
>
> "Oh, wicked, wicked!" gasped the elder, "may the Lord deliver us from evil!"

This is in retaliation for Joseph's ' "yah're a nowt . . . yah'll . . . goa raight tuh t'divil, like yer mother afore ye!" ', and it sends Joseph off in a genuine fright. Cathy adroitly travesties him, with a witty vindictiveness which does indeed prove she is her mother's daughter; the author casts some doubt on the Black Art by associating it with the mockery of such easy targets as Joseph, not to mention red cows and rheumatism. Yet Lockwood with deep unease has no idea where he is or what is going on; this victim of our laughter is stirred by a contagious fear as he tries to penetrate the darkness. We in our turn puzzle over the slatternly, golden-haired girl who is at once witch and, ironically, 'good fairy',

'beneficent fairy', and not less as we come through the novel to
find her exercising a benign sexual magic on Hareton, leading him
out of the dark. It is possible for readers to credit the continuing
power of her mother buried in the moorland which has its own
underlying and spell-binding magic powers. Nelly too is rooted in
this tradition: these roots in her Yorkshire home are the source of
her second sight. Book-learning and sociable living among the
gentry have not managed to erase superstitions gathered from the
cradle onward, though she eternally fusses to repress them with a
weight of sound sense and Christian pieties. Through her fancy
that the elf-child Hindley looked at her, Emily Brontë suggests the
possible but not demonstrable presence of an adjacent reality
through which a link passes to connect humanity, the earth and
the spirit of the earth. 'The child lifted its face . . . it vanished'.
Here is the 'it' of the child which is feared by the adult world for its
a-social, a-rational and a-moral characteristics, somehow pre-
human and alien like the cuckoo in the nest which every child to
some degree impersonates; the 'it' of an elf whose unknown
powers are probably malevolent; the 'it' of nature herself,
inhuman and incomprehensible. These are mirrors carrying one
another's reflection. When Nelly arrives at the Heights after her
waking dream, she sets eyes on a little boy whom she cannot
distinguish from the vision of Hindley:

> The apparition had outstripped me; it stood looking through
> the gate. That was my first idea on observing an elf-locked,
> brown-eyed boy setting his ruddy countenance against the
> bars. Further reflection suggested this must be Hareton, *my*
> Hareton, not altered greatly since I left him, ten months
> since.

Nelly is beginning to find difficulty in separating out the layers of
reality. Past and present, father and son, have become
indecipherable. Catherine has already gestured toward this
identity when she remarked on Hindley's fatherhood of the baby
Hareton, ' "how sweetly his father curses in his solitude! You
remember him, I dare say, when he was just such another as that
chubby thing—nearly as young and innocent." ' Hareton
reproduces his father's child-image, to the life, for he too is 'it', his
hair 'elf-locked', but his cheeks are naturalistically and
reassuringly ruddy with outdoor health. Nelly is muddled, and

has to straighten herself out with a dose of rational reflection to make a correct identification of the strange boy. In another sense though, her muddle yields a deep and true perception. She sees through to the fact that we reflect each other. When we crack the code of individual names, labels, clothings, behaviours—the film of eccentricity upon the surface—there is an identity so fundamental that we 'are' one another. The child Hareton repeats the child Hindley as Cathy repeats Catherine; but even more powerfully Hareton repeats the child Heathcliff, as his shadow or double. This is amusingly revealed in Hareton's response to Nelly's ecstatic greeting:

> "God bless thee, darling! . . . Hareton, it's Nelly—Nelly, thy nurse."
> He retreated out of arm's length, and picked up a large flint.

Heathcliff, having had charge of Hareton for ten months, has had time to remake him in his own image, as an inveterate infant hooligan who bombards his ex-nurse with missiles and lets loose a volley of curses at her. Nelly looks infinitely foolish as she launches a doting speech of baby-talk at this vandal. It is a case of mistaken identity just as surely as Lockwood's misbegotten guesses at the relationships at the Heights, with Cathy as Hareton's 'amiable lady' and at the second throw (an unconscious prediction) Hareton's 'beneficent fairy'. The twin narrators, asking questions or making assumptions on our behalf, are stoned by the jeers or missiles of the protagonists they try to name, and by our laughter at their expense.

For Nelly, it is more painful. The Hareton who has learned to speak only to have his baby mouth filled with curses, who hates 'Devil daddy' in whose likeness he so uncannily appears, was her own foster-baby. She participates both in surface farce and in the losses which are sustained by so many of the characters in the novel. She is forgotten by Hareton, her imprint deleted. The author refers to the myth of the fall. Nelly gets an orange out of her pocket, to bribe the surly boy to explain his condition. Greedily, he jumps and grabs at the fruit. As Hareton in his innocence was one with his father as a child, so he shares the fallen condition of Hindley and Heathcliff, scarred and thwarted. Nelly removes herself smartly, 'feeling as scared as if I had reared a goblin.' The toddler has forgotten that he was ever in the Eden of Nelly's loving care. Yet this innocence is not as lost as Nelly thinks, and the second Cathy's loving education of Hareton toward the close of the book explicitly reclaims the garden of Wuthering Heights, not for the growth of any potentially fatal fruit—she gets Hareton to clear Joseph's currant and gooseberry bushes which were, in a witty pun, 'the apple of Joseph's eye'—but to plant a useless flower-bed. According to Joseph, who is even more than commonly irate:

> "shoo's taan my garden frough me, un' by th' heart! Maister, Aw cannot stand it! . . .
> "Its yon flaysome, graceless quean, ut's witched ahr lad, wi' her bold een, un' her forrard ways—till—Nay! It fair brusts my heart! He's forgotten all E done for him, un' made on him, un' goan un' riven up a whole row ut t' grandest currant trees, i' t' garden!"

The southern middle-class reader only with difficulty spells out the sound and meaning of Joseph's dialect speeches. Yet, though they are in the tightest code of all, the reader has the key and can persevere until the joke dawns and then shines fully upon her or him. Joseph, the fool on the heath, is the most indigenous and rooted in the world of the Heights: as he was there in the beginning, so he will be left there at the end. Unbearable as he is in his sanctified spleen, he is the least dispensable person to the fictional world, rooting it down to the real Yorkshire, standing for a whole tradition of religious dissent degenerated into claptrap, but also for the fierce vigour of northern dialect which is a proudly different language from 'standard' English. He is there to be laughed at. But he is also there to laugh at you, with your surface polish of class (' "feared uh muckying yer grand silk cloes" '), your precious and affected southern dialect (' "I wish to see my bed-room". *Bed-rume*! . . . Yah's see all t' *Bed-rumes* thear is . . ." '). Joseph stands for reality.

But it is reality under the old dispensation—an Old Testament reality. He complains dourly about his garden which has been partially uprooted by an alien female intruder—' "shoo's taan my garden frough me" '. As a dark, parody shadow to Heathcliff, his master, he makes it possible for the author to hint at a reversal of the Eden legend. He implies that Cathy is a new Eve inciting her mate to rebellion, and claims to be suffering himself from this 'bold' and 'forrard' tendency in woman. Joseph, the only representative of dogmatic Christian religion in the novel, implies that Heathcliff is the creator of a sort of Adam in Hareton (' "He's forgetten all E . . . made on him" '), whose purity has been corrupted by the usurping, spell-binding Cathy. But Cathy and Hareton, unlike Eve and Adam, have not yielded to a tame dare to eat the fruit and see what happens. Emily Brontë's Eve digs the garden up by the roots, takes it over, and replants it with stocks and wall-flowers, emblems not so much of domestication as of the fertility of the future. In the face of the apparently omnipotent Heathcliff, she is daredevil, 'returning his angry glare, and, meantime, biting a crust, the remnant of her breakfast'. This adolescent gesture stabilizes the 'mythical' element, but we hear the resonance of the Eden expulsion again as Heathcliff threatens Hareton with exile from his lands:

> "As to Hareton Earnshaw, if I see him listen to you, I'll send him seeking his bread where he can get it! Your love will make him an outcast, and a beggar—"

The terribly cursing God of Genesis is echoed here:

> Because thou hast hearkened unto the voice of thy wife . . .
> cursed is the ground for thy sake . . .
> In the sweat of thy face shalt thou eat bread, till thou return unto the ground . . .
> So he drove out the man . . .

But the implication of *Wuthering Heights* is that man may not rightfully be dispossessed of his inheritance in the Eden of his childhood intuitions and affinities. Cathy, who is accused of causing Hareton to be 'an outcast, and a beggar', exemplifies not an irresponsible Eve's black arts but a female white magic which acts to reclaim first happiness. She plants a new garden and liberates man from the old (we remember the infant Hareton staring out balefully from behind the bars of the gate, as if from a prison); she educates and humanizes, by drawing forth the tender and liberal child-spirit and cultivating it. Finally, she restores his own lands to him, and joins her own with them. Emily Brontë celebrates the harmonious union of like with like, according to a reconciling principle which draws power not from a patriarchal code but from a descent which is matriarchal and matrilinear. Nelly sits looking on at Hareton and Cathy reading together, toward the end of the novel, with an increasingly soothed feeling that derives from the sense that 'they both appeared, in a measure, my children'. There is a qualification in the phrase 'in a measure' since, as she goes on to meditate, these 'twinned' cousins are linked by a more organic inheritance than anything she could have fostered:

> They lifted their eyes together, to encounter Mr Heathcliff—perhaps you have never remarked that their eyes are precisely similar, and they are those of Catherine Earnshaw. The present Catherine has no other likeness to her. . . . With Hareton the resemblance is carried further: it is singular, at all times. . . .

The eyes are by an ancient tradition the windows of the soul, and the dominant features of the face. As first cousins, Cathy and Hareton inherit not just the 'Earnshaw' eyes but, explicitly, '*Catherine* Earnshaw's' eyes, to the confounding of the science of genetics, and according to the benignly shaping power exercised by that bias which is eternally present in the world of *Wuthering Heights* as 'the mother beneath the earth'.